Prayer:

Insights from St Thérèse of Lisieux

CHRISTOPHER O'DONNELL OCARM

Published by
Veritas Publications
7/8 Lower Abbey Street
Dublin 1
Ireland

Email: publications@veritas.ie
Website: http://www.veritas.ie

ISBN 1 85390 587 9

British Library Cataloguing
in Publication Data.
A catalogue record for
this book is available
from the British Library.

Cover design by Bill Bolger
Printed in the Republic of Ireland by Betaprint Ltd, Dublin

Veritas books are printed on paper made from the wood pulp of managed forests. For every tree felled, at least one tree is planted, thereby renewing natural resources.

Contents

This book celebrates the visit of the relics of
St Thérèse of Lisieux to Ireland in April-June 2001

Acknowledgements

The author wishes to thank the following:

St Thérèse herself.
V. Rev. J. Linus Ryan OCarm, long a friend of Thérèse, the main organiser
of the visit of the relics, and all those who worked with him.
Sr Máire O'Donnell RSHM and Sr Áine Hayde HFB, astute readers who
provided suggestions, help and encouragement.
Aideen Quigley, editor in Veritas, keen-eyed and very patient.

Abbreviations and Texts of Thérèse

FRENCH TEXTS:

Concord   Sr Geneviève et al. *Les mots de sainte Thérèse de l'Enfant-Jésus et de la Sainte-Face: Concordance générale* (Paris: Éditions du Cerf, 1996).
A concordance of her works.

CritEd   *Histoire d'une âme de Sainte Thérèse de Lisieux selon la disposition originale des autographes nouvellement établie par Conrad De Meester* (Moerzeke, Belgium: Carmel-EdiT, 1999).
A new critical edition of her autobiography.

OeuvC   *Oeuvres complètes* (Paris: Éditions du Cerf – Desclée de Brouwer, 1992). Complete works in French.

PO and PA: *Procès de béatification et canonisation de sainte Thérèse de l'Enfant-Jésus et de la Sainte-Face.* Vol. 1 – *Procès informatif ordinaire;* Vol. 2 – *Procès apostolique* (Rome: Teresianum, 1973, 1976). The documentation for her beatification and canonisation.

ENGLISH TRANSLATIONS

CS   Sr Geneviève of the Holy Face (Céline Martin), *My Sister Saint Thérèse* (Rockford, Ill: Tan Books, 1997) Translation of *Conseils et Souvenirs.*
The chapter number is given first, followed by page number in English/French books.

LastConv

Her Last Conversations. Translated by J. Clarke (Washington: Institute of Carmelite Studies, 1977).
The day, month and entry are given from the French edition, followed by page numbers in Clarke translation and in OeuvC.

Letters

Letters of Saint Thérèse of Lisieux. Translated by J. Clarke. 2 vols. (Washington: Institute of Carmelite Studies, 1982, 1988).
The date of each letter is given followed by the enumeration LT 1–266 of the French edition. The volume and page numbers in the Clarke translation and in the OeuvC are given.

O'Mahony

St Thérèse of Lisieux by Those Who Knew Her. Translated and edited by C. O'Mahony (Dublin: Veritas, 1975).
Mostly texts from the diocesan inquiry (PO) above.

PN and PS

The Poetry of Saint Thérèse of Lisieux. Translated by D. Kinney (Washington: Institute of Carmelite Studies, 1995).
The French poem number is given (PN 1–54 for main collection and PS 1–8 for supplementary poems), followed by the stanza, the page numbers in Kinney translation and in OeuvC.

Pri

The Prayers of Saint Thérèse of Lisieux. Translated by A. Kane (Washington: Institute of Carmelite Studies, 1997).
The French prayer number is given (Pri 1–21), followed by page numbers in Kane translation and in OeuvC.

RP   The eight Pious Recreations – dramatic pieces written by Thérèse for performance at community feasts. English translation is forthcoming.

The French number of the piece (RP 1–8) is given followed by manuscript indications and page number in OeuvC.

SSoul   *Story of a Soul: The Autobiography of St Thérèse of Lisieux.* Translated by J. Clarke (Washington: Institute of Carmelite Studies, 3rd edition, 1996). The traditional chapter number is given first, followed by page number. The manuscript number and page reference is given from OeuvC (A, B, C) and from the critical edition (A[gnes], G[ongague] and M[arie]), followed by the page numbers of OeuvC and CritEd. For example, SSoul ch. 11, 243/Ms C-G 25r, OeuvC 268/CritEd 287 is a passage from the traditional chapter eleven found in Clarke translation on page 243. The French is from Ms C of the older versions, Ms G of the critical edition – both of course in Thérèse's hand-written text on the front page of leaf 25 of manuscript copybook. The passage is on page 268 of the French complete works, and on page 287 of the critical edition.

Thérèse was very fond of capitalisation, underlining, ellipsis points (. . .) and exclamations. These are reproduced in citations from her works, with underlining being replaced by italics. Where ellipsis points are enclosed in square brackets [. . .], the author has abbreviated the citation, leaving out one sentence or more – these ellipses points are not Thérèse's.

1

A Teacher of Prayer

All who write on the spiritual life agree on the need for prayer. Yet one will seldom meet people who are satisfied with the way they pray. Most feel that there is some method, some special way that leads to that ideal prayer, which continues to elude them: a feeling that others seem to have it but not me. Hence the popularity of books on prayer. We buy them hoping that this will be the one that will finally open the gate to praying properly.

It is not, however, easy to know what to say to people who state, 'My prayer is not going well.' For one thing, we might wonder what they mean, and if there is a deeper problem lurking behind the dissatisfaction with the effort of praying. We might wonder how they are attempting to pray. Many people might be at a loss if asked, 'What would your prayer be like if it were better?'

Prayer and love
There is a danger of getting a distorted emphasis in the spiritual life. Should our primary focus be on prayer at all? The two great commandments do not mention prayer: 'You shall love the Lord your God with all your heart, and with all your soul, and with all your strength, and with all your mind; and your neighbour as yourself' (Lk 10:27). Perhaps prayer is one of the ways in which we fulfil the double command of love. Maybe it is not possible to satisfy the command of Jesus to love God and our neighbour unless we pray. It might even be argued that through prayer the observance of the commandments is possible.[1] Instead of seeing prayer as an area in which we fail, we should rather see prayer as probably indispensable, if we are to come into full authenticity as human persons.

If prayer is an expression of love that makes love possible, then it is more important that we keep our eyes fixed on God and on our neighbour, than that we focus too narrowly on the health of our prayer and its soundness. It might then follow that our notion of God and our concern for neighbour will determine the soundness of our prayer. Who anyway is the God we pray to? A fixer, a judge, an all-seeing policeman, a parent, a lover . . ? Depending on how we see God, our prayer can be selfish, anxious, fearful, guilt-ridden, loving, filled with amazement, wonder, praise and thanksgiving . . . The Book of Psalms shows us much of the vast range of prayer and its many forms.

Some difficulties

We are right to be concerned about prayer. St Paul tells us, 'pray without ceasing' (1 Thess 5:17). This injunction seems scarcely possible. And there are other problems. The comment of St John of the Cross is surely worrying: 'Many individuals think they are not praying when, indeed, their prayer is deep. Others place high value on their prayer while it amounts to little more than nothing.'[2]

Yet very few of the enormous number of books on prayer in recent years give much guidance on what is surely a crucial problem: are we praying at all? St John of the Cross would seem to focus rather little on prayer: his four great treatises and incomparable poetry are not so much about prayer as about love. Similarly surprising is his contemporary, St Teresa of Avila. In her most mature work, *The Interior Castle,* she sets out in obedience to ecclesiastical superiors to write a book on prayer, yet much of this book seems concerned not so much with prayer as with spiritual growth.[3] We would still resist the suggestion that prayer and spiritual growth are the same: spiritual growth is ultimately about love.

St Thérèse

What would the newest Doctor of the Church, St Thérèse of Lisieux, say to those who are unhappy with their prayer and who may be confused by so much talk? She certainly shared at times our feeling that the way we pray is inadequate. But the difference between her and us may lie in the fact that, for Thérèse and the saints, prayer is insufficient and incomplete because God is infinite and beyond our human language, indeed beyond our human hearts. But many of us look at our prayer rather than at God. Thérèse can at once set us free from undue trepidation about prayer and point us towards God and our neighbour in a way that can transform our attempts to pray. Since she has given the Church her 'Little Way' of holiness, might she not also show us a simple way of prayer?

It seems that she does. *The Catechism of the Catholic Church* prefaces its treatment of the question, 'What is prayer?' with a quotation from St Thérèse: 'For me, prayer is a surge of the heart; it is a simple look turned towards heaven, it is a cry of recognition and love, embracing both trial and joy.'[4]

This would seem to be a very simple, straightforward and indeed encouraging view of prayer. But the same *Catechism* that gives special prominence to this text of Thérèse goes on to speak of prayer in 307 articles spread over 66 pages. And it has already devoted 15 pages and 73 articles to liturgy, during which it deals with the great prayer of the Church: the Liturgy of the Hours.[5] The *Catechism* is very comprehensive, treating of various expressions of the life of prayer – prayer in Scripture, kinds of prayer, the tradition of prayer, the life of prayer, with various expressions and difficulties of prayer. We could be excused for wondering where the consoling text of Thérèse had gone: 'a surge of the heart . . . a simple look . . . a cry of recognition.' Having given us encouragement in Thérèse, the *Catechism* might seem to confirm our worst fears that prayer is complicated, abstruse, and quite beyond us.

We know that a catalyst in the discovery of the Little Way was Thérèse's great desire to be holy, which appeared frustrated by her feeling that she could not imitate the great saints. We find something similar about prayer. Towards the end of her life she confesses that she felt overwhelmed by the many beautiful prayers that were available to her:

> Outside the Divine Office, which I am very unworthy to recite, I do not have the courage to force myself to search out beautiful prayers in books. There are so many of them it really gives me a headache! And each prayer is more beautiful than the others. I cannot recite them all and not knowing which to

choose, I do like children who do not know how to read, I say very simply to God what I wish to say, without composing beautiful sentences, and He always understands me.

She then goes on to give her idea of prayer, which we quoted earlier.[6]

This text of Thérèse, used so prominently in the *Catechism* and to which we shall return later, is from the last six months of her life. It is from a time of deep spiritual darkness. It might be said to sum up her idea of prayer, and it certainly supports the suspicion that there might be a Little Way of prayer. It has often been remarked that whereas Thérèse's Little Way is simple, it is by no means easy. Thérèse herself walked along it to the point of heroism. Likewise we might find Thérèse's way of prayer simple too. It remains to be seen if it is easy.

In Thérèse as in her spiritual mother, the sixteenth-century St Teresa of Avila, we can see a life of prayer, a doctrine of prayer and practical teaching about prayer. She is not as systematic as the Reformer of Carmel. In the case of the great Teresa of Avila, circumstances and Church authorities led her to attempt some coherent and reasonably systematic account of prayer. Thérèse's writings are much more occasional and she does not set out to give any methodical treatment of prayer. But prayer is quite central in her writings. She uses the word 'prayer' (*prière*) 167 times in her own writings; it is found 6 times in her recorded *Last Conversations;* the verb 'to pray' (*prier*) is found 274 times and 26 times respectively.[7]

We can nonetheless find her a teacher of prayer for our time. Firstly, we can study her life and writings to see how she prayed. Implicit in what she writes about prayer and in the prayers that she has left is a doctrine about prayer. Secondly, we can attempt to see how she understands prayer. Thirdly, we can learn practical ways of prayer from her. But though these three points are helpful to orient ourselves to our topic of Prayer and Thérèse, they must not be too narrowly considered. We must also be on guard against the twofold danger of reading into Thérèse what she never intended, and of distorting her teaching. One way of avoiding any twisting of her thought will be to give ample quotations, thus allowing her to speak in her own words.

An exposition of Thérèse's doctrine on prayer is long overdue. Though there are some excellent short essays in other languages[8] and many writers devote some space to her prayer, we are still without a lengthy study in English.

The prayer of St Thérèse

An obvious approach to the prayer of St Thérèse is to examine its evolution throughout her life. This method has been adopted in some important accounts of her prayer.[9] It is obviously important to consider her prayer before she entered Carmel as well as her mature views. In this present study we will outline the major stages of her development in prayer (chapter 2) before going on to consider its Carmelite foundations (chapter 3). Chapters follow on the Liturgy of the Hours, the Eucharist, mental prayer, vocal prayer and the prayers she composed. Finally, we will consider her ongoing contribution as a teacher of prayer for the Church.

2

A Life of Continual Prayer

One has only to dip anywhere into the writings of Thérèse to see that hers was a life of continual prayer. She constantly speaks about prayer. Like Teresa of Avila, who obviously influenced her here, she frequently breaks into prayer even as she writes her autobiography or when in correspondence with her family and friends. Her poems and the prayers that she wrote all point to prayer as a central feature of her life. It will obviously be valuable to see her life in two stages: before and after she entered Carmel. But this second period needs to be studied against the great graces and insights that she received in the convent. We begin with what was her greatest formative influence – her home at Les Buissonnets.

Before she entered Carmel
The family home of St Thérèse was nothing if not devout.[1] Indeed, to our mentality it might even seem stifling. Both her parents, Louis and Zélie Martin, had thought of becoming religious in their youth. As a married couple they never lost their deep faith and piety. Pope John Paul II declared them both Venerable on 26 March 1994, which is the first step towards beatification. This action also involves a judgement by the Church that their lives were marked by heroic virtue.

Thérèse's parents were accustomed to attend daily Mass at 5.30 in the morning. The family observed strict fasting and there was prayer each day and devout reading. They were especially marked by their love and generosity towards those who were poor or in need.

Thérèse's mother never enjoyed good health, eventually succumbing to cancer when Thérèse was four. Even in these early years, her mother's letters give many indications of Thérèse's simple piety. The family moved to Lisieux after Zélie Martin's death. There

the same rhythm of life was taken up again. Soon the girls would
daily accompany their father to the 6.00 or 7.00 morning Mass.
Louis Martin was devoted to the Rosary. He was also a member of
the local St Vincent de Paul Conference. He had an upper room,
called the Belvedere, where he spent much time alone in prayer and
reflection. There was daily family prayer, readings from spiritual
books, notably the recently published classic of Dom Guéranger, *The
Liturgical Year.* Thérèse would later recall the joy of celebrating
Sundays, the great feasts, Eucharistic processions and May
devotions.[2] Louis Martin liked to visit churches in his daily walk,
usually accompanied by Thérèse. The paper bought by Mr Martin
was the Catholic *La Croix,* but only the older daughters were allowed
to read it. The home was very much a Catholic one with all the
symbols, prayers and outlook that one associates with late
nineteenth-century French religiosity. All of this is the background
for any consideration of prayer in Thérèse's early life.

Her early prayers

There is some difficulty in grasping the content and evaluating
Thérèse's early prayer. There are references in her mother's letters that
would seem to suggest some rather precocious devotion. We have
Thérèse's own account of her youth, but this is written in her
spiritual maturity, less than three years before her death, and when
she had already discovered her Little Way. We have then to be alert
to the fact that we have some perhaps unconscious editing of her
memories as she reflects later on her childhood experiences of God
and of prayer.

A key to any grasp of Thérèse's prayer is her sense of relationship
with God. The family was brought up in the French tradition of
'practices', that is, making little sacrifices or small acts of virtue that
expressed love for God or were offered in intercession for others.[3]
Thérèse took up such little sacrifices at a very early age. She
redoubled her practices in preparation for her First Communion by
performing acts and saying aspirations. She called this gathering fresh
flowers for Jesus;[4] within sixty-eight days she had totalled 1,949 little
acts.[5] From late infancy she was desirous of loving and serving God.

She remarked that from an early age she seriously tried to cultivate
virtue, even though at that time goodness coexisted with immaturity
and selfishness:

> As I had an excessive *self-love* and also a *love* of the *good*, as soon
> as I began to think seriously (which I did when still very little),
> it was enough for one to tell me a thing wasn't good and I had
> no desire to repeat it twice.[6]

Thinking about that period of her life she remarked:

> Virtue had its charming qualities for me, and I was, it seems to
> me, in the same dispositions then as I am now, enjoying a firm
> control over my actions.[7]

She would later remark that, at about the age of ten, when she
encountered flattery, she could have fallen into vanity and that the
Lord's mercy protected her: 'However, if my heart *had not been raised
to God from the dawn of reason*, if the world had smiled on me from
my entrance into life, what would have become of me?'[8] Such a
concern to do what is right, though admirable, could well have led to
a cold, juridical service of God. But Thérèse was protected from any
such deviation by her image of God, which was deeply influenced by
that of her father; knowing the doting love of her father led Thérèse
easily to accept the notion of God's deep personal love for her. In turn
she wanted to please God. Her father's personality and life were a
decisive influence on her, and nurtured her image of and relationship
with God. Recalling the family prayers, said before the statue of Our
Lady of the Smile, Thérèse spoke of only 'having to look at him to
see how the saints prayed'.[9]

There were family events that led to a deepened love of God and
attachment to prayer. The first reception of Confession and
Communion of her sisters Pauline and Marie made a deep
impression on Thérèse. She would naturally have wished to share
their grace. Instead, she had to be content to wait whilst sharing their
joy. When she was too young to go to Mass she delighted to share in
the blessed bread distributed at High Mass.[10]

Her sisters

Thérèse's sisters had a very profound influence on her whole upbringing. It would be beyond the scope of this study to evaluate these influences. Pauline was an early favourite. When their mother died, Céline chose Marie as a 'second mother', while Thérèse chose Pauline, who was twelve years older than her. Pauline entered Carmel when Thérèse was nine, becoming Sr Agnes of Jesus. But she continued to be a key role model for Thérèse. Later she was Thérèse's prioress, and she recorded the *Last Conversations,* sayings from Thérèse's final months. The eldest sister was Marie, thirteen years older than Thérèse. She became Thérèse's 'third mother' after Pauline entered the Carmel. Marie prepared her for the sacraments of Confession and Communion and guided her with great delicacy and skill in the bad period of scrupulosity when Thérèse was twelve and thirteen. She left for Carmel when Thérèse was thirteen. Later, in the convent, there was some reversal of roles, as Thérèse became a model and teacher for Marie. Léonie, two years younger than Pauline, was a child with special needs.[11] Emotionally very handicapped, she was given to violent and strange behaviour. She tried her religious vocation several times, before eventually being accepted as a Visitation Sister after Thérèse's death. The family loved Léonie, but skills for helping such a person were not known then. Eventually she came into healing, living with great holiness in the Visitation convent at Caen. There is little hint in Thérèse's writings of the difficulty and tensions that must have been caused by Léonie's tantrums. Thérèse does occasionally speak of 'poor Léonie,' especially in the context of her failed attempts at religious life. For two critical years before she entered, Thérèse had as her companion Céline, four years her senior.

The bonding of these two youngest was very close. At Céline's First Communion, Thérèse recalls having a heavy heart, as she had to wait four years more. But she goes on:

> The day of Céline's First Communion left me with an impression similar to my own First Communion. When awakening in the morning all alone in the big bed, I felt *inundated with joy.* 'It's today! The great day has arrived.' I repeated this over and over again. It seemed it was I who was

going to make my First Communion. I believe I received great graces that day and I consider it one of the most beautiful in my life.[12]

From the age of fourteen Thérèse enjoyed a deepened communion of thoughts and experiences with her beloved Céline. She likened their conversations to the famous description by St Augustine of his dialogue with his mother:

> I don't know if I'm mistaken, but it seems to me the outpourings of our souls were similar to those of St Monica with her son when, at the port of Ostia, they were lost in ecstasy at the sight of the Creator's marvels! It appears we were receiving graces like those granted to the great saints . . . how *light* and *transparent* the veil was which hid Jesus from our gaze. [. . .] Graces as great as this were not to be without fruit and it was abundant. The practice of virtue became sweet and natural to us. At the beginning, it is true, my face betrayed the struggle, but little by little this vanished and renunciation became easy . . . [13]

Later, speaking of her own proposed entry to Carmel, which caused Céline great pain, Thérèse commented: 'To understand how great it was, one would have to know how close we were. It was, so to speak, the same soul giving us life.'[14] Céline, with great generosity, supported Thérèse's desire to enter Carmel, even though she too had the same desire, but remained to look after their father and Léonie.[15] This intimacy with Céline grew and is reflected in some of Thérèse's finest letters, in which she shares her deepest thoughts about her vocation. Thérèse may well have been able to share more deeply with Céline in letters than with Marie and Pauline in the more formal encounters of Carmel.

A contemplative child

One cannot but be struck by an aspect of Thérèse's personality that we can in a wide sense call 'contemplative'. This emerges from an early age. She certainly was at times dreamy, liking solitude or the company of only a small few. But this natural reserve, and her pleasure at being alone with her thoughts, in time opened up to genuine religious reflection and prayer. She recalled that when her father went fishing, she occasionally tried with her own little line,

> but I preferred to go *alone* and sit on the grass bedecked with flowers, and then my thoughts became very profound indeed! Without knowing what it was to meditate, my soul was absorbed in real prayer. . . . I listened to distant sounds, the murmuring of the wind. . . . Earth then seemed to be a place of exile and I could dream only of heaven.[16]

This is surely a somewhat idealised interpretation, but it is not unique. Many similar ideas are found in her childhood reminiscences. She recalls her rapt contemplation of stars,[17] her first sight of the sea when she was six or seven: 'I couldn't take my eyes off it since its majesty, the roaring of its waves, everything spoke to my soul of God's grandeur and power.'[18] The beauties of nature seen on her pilgrimage with her father and Céline to Rome at the age of fourteen drew her to contemplate the Creator.[19]

Again, outside the classroom where she shone, Thérèse could be described as a misfit at school. She was not comfortable in her interaction with the other children, especially at playtime. A game she remembered especially was playing hermits, vowed to silence, with her cousin Marie Guérin.[20] A further difficulty arose from the fact that after her First Communion she noticed that the other children did not share her values and those of her family. Since she did not know how to play the games of her companions, she tells us, 'often during the recreations, I leaned against a tree and studied my companions at a distance, giving myself to serious reflections!' or she told stories, which other children gathered around to hear.[21]

She was moved by religious pictures, spending hours looking at them. During her retreat in preparation for her First Communion, Céline sent her a holy picture 'The Little Flower of the Divine Prisoner'. She remarked, 'How many thoughts of love had I not experienced through it.' Again she wrote that this picture 'said so many things to me that I became deeply recollected'.[22]

Her early attachment to the spiritual classic, *The Imitation of Christ* by Thomas á Kempis, should be noted in this context:

> I was nourished for a long time on the 'pure flour' contained
> in the *Imitation of Christ* this being the only book that did me
> any good, for as yet I had not discovered the treasures hidden
> in the Gospels. I knew almost all the chapters of my beloved
> *Imitation* by heart. This little book never parted company with
> me.[23]

By the age of fourteen she knew the chapters almost by heart. The *Imitation of Christ* is less popular now than it was. To many today it seems dry and hard, unrelenting in its demands. But it is precisely this book that Thérèse treasured not only in adulthood, but also in childhood. It gives a corrective to any notion we might entertain of Thérèse as engaged in dreamy spiritual escapism. When she was fourteen she read the book of the Abbé Arminjon, *The End of the Present World and the Mysteries of the Future Life,* which the Carmel had lent to her father. This had a deep effect on her:

> All the great truths of religion, the mysteries of eternity,
> plunged my soul into a state of joy not of this earth. . . . I
> wanted *to love, to love Jesus with a passion,* giving Him a
> thousand proofs of my love while it was possible. I copied out
> several passages on perfect love, on the reception God will give
> His Elect at the moment He becomes their Reward, great and
> eternal, and I repeated over and over the words of love burning
> in my heart.[24]

A remark that she made about her dispositions possibly at the age of six is very significant: 'I loved God very much and offered my heart to him very often, making use of the little formula Mother had taught me.' This prayer was, 'My God I give you my heart; take it please so that no creature may possess it, but you alone good Jesus.'[25] Already we see hints of that single-minded girl who treasured the stern *Imitation of Christ.*

There are also indications that she was not only thoughtful and introspective, but that her times of silence were given to genuine reflective prayer. She remarked that when she was about ten she was thinking about her future entry into Carmel:

> I was thinking things over in my *bed* (for it was there I made my profound meditations, and contrary to the bride in the Canticles, I always found my Beloved there). . .[26]

It is significant that the word translated here as 'meditations' is *oraisons*, generally used for mental prayer. Still clearer is a key text as she reflects about the time of her First Communion:

> At this time in my life nobody had ever taught me how to make mental prayer [*oraison*], and yet I had a great desire to make it. Marie, finding me pious enough, allowed me to make only my vocal prayers. One day, one of my teachers at the Abbey asked me what I did on my free afternoons when I was alone. I told her I went behind my bed in an empty space that was there, and that it was easy to close myself with my bedcurtain and that '*I thought*.' 'But what do you think about?' she asked. 'I think about God, about life, about ETERNITY . . . I *think!*' The good religious laughed heartily at me, and later on she loved reminding me of the time when I *thought*, asking me if I *was still thinking*. I understand now that I was making mental prayer [*je faisais oraison*] without knowing it and God was already instructing me in secret.[27]

We cannot dismiss this liking for recollection as mere dreaminess, though this was surely also present. It is found within a context of seeking virtue and a love of prayer. Like her father, she delighted in the things of God. Of all her lessons she liked catechism and study of the bible or sacred history best. She was distressed, which may well have included some wounded pride, when she failed to obtain the best mark in class because she was unable to name the father of Moses (Amram, Ex 6:20!).[28]

Another sign of the basic solidity of her spiritual life during her childhood is the presence of dryness and darkness in it. This is a topic to be examined later, but we can briefly note her bitter disappointment when her formidable uncle, Isidore Guérin, did not agree to her entering Carmel when she was fifteen. Even though Thérèse's father was still alive, his brother was a surrogate guardian for his children. As such, his consent was necessary for Thérèse's entry. From the time of her father's mental illness in 1889 until his death in 1894 the influence of Isidore on the family increased. He was an astute businessman, a journalist, a politician and a great benefactor of the Lisieux Carmel; later he would see to the first publication of her autobiography, *The Story of a Soul.* But at this stage Isidore was the cause of much pain for Thérèse, as she recalled, 'my heart plunged into the most profound bitterness. My only consolation was prayer.'[29]   Uncle Isidore was quickly converted to Thérèse's cause and soon withdrew his opposition to her entering at the age of fifteen.

Four significant experiences
The remainder of this book will mainly be an examination of Thérèse's prayer in Carmel. But it is important to note four great moments in her life that deeply influenced her prayer and her understanding of it. We leave aside her Christmas conversion when she was thirteen. Until then she was often touchy and tearful. On Christmas Eve, she overheard an irritable remark of her father. This time she did not cry. Though Thérèse rightly sees it as one of the greatest blessings in her life, when she was healed of childish ways in an instant, we do not have very much certain or direct evidence about how it influenced her prayer. It certainly matured her and made possible her entry to Carmel two years later in 1888. The four other experiences had a more direct and discernible effect on her prayer. Indeed we should be alert to passages in her writings that come after these since they represent her mature thought.

The first was her discovery of the Little Way in autumn 1894. After the death of their father in July that year, Céline quickly made her way to the Lisieux Carmel. She brought with her a notebook in which she had copied out passages from the Old Testament – a book to which Thérèse had no access. When Céline gave Thérèse this notebook, she discovered two texts that would be decisive for her grasp of the Little Way of spiritual childhood, which she described as an elevator to bring her to God. She had wanted to be a saint, but the ways of the saints seemed beyond her. She said:

> Instead of being discouraged, I said to myself: God cannot inspire unrealisable desires. I can, then, in spite of my littleness, aspire to holiness. It is impossible for me to grow up, and so I must bear with myself such as I am with all my imperfections. But I want to seek out a means of going to heaven by a little way, a way that is very straight, very short and totally new.

She realised that the elevator she needed was the arms of Jesus, and she concludes,

> And for this I had no need to grow up, but rather I had to remain little and remain this more and more.[30]

After this she made profound discoveries about the nature of practical love in community and of the importance of little things offered to God in love. This discovery by Thérèse has been recounted by herself in her autobiography[31] and innumerable times by others.[32]

The second experience was her self-offering to God's merciful love in June 1895. We shall examine this prayer in a later chapter. Thérèse had a deep sense that, of all the divine attributes, the merciful love of God was not acknowledged or given full reign in creation. Suffice for now to note its date: she offered herself to Merciful Love on Trinity Sunday, 9 June 1895, making a formal Act a few days later with Céline. After making it she said that 'rivers or rather oceans of graces' flooded her soul:

> Ah! since that happy day, it seems to me that *Love* penetrates and surrounds me, that at each moment this *Merciful Love* renews me, purifying my soul and leaving no trace of sin within it.[33]

The third experience was an entry into what she called, 'the deepest darkness,' a trial of faith that would last from Easter 1896 until her death eighteen months later. This matter will be treated later, but for the moment we can note that some of her most radiant and intense writing comes from this most painful time of darkness.

During that period of trial she came into her discovery of the profound meaning of her vocation, which was to be 'love in the heart of the Church' and can be dated to July/August 1896. This overmastering insight led to the new depths in her understanding of practical love, which we find in the closing pages of that part of her autobiography addressed to Mother Gonzaga (MS C and G).

Prayer in Carmel

Thérèse quickly settled into the routine of Carmel. Though it was decided that she should not enter until after Lent in 1888, the daily timetable was still very demanding for a fifteen-year-old. Rising was at 5.45 a.m. in winter (4.45 in summer) and the sisters retired at 10.30 p.m. In summer there was a possible siesta or rest period for an hour at noon. Meals were at 10.00 a.m. and 6.00 p.m. There were two hours of community sharing and five hours of manual work. The total time of prayer in choir was six hours. Mass with thanksgiving was nearly an hour. There were two hours of personal mental prayer. The Divine Office/Liturgy of the Hours on some days took almost three hours. There was also a twice-daily ten-minute examination of conscience and thirty minutes of spiritual reading.

We get the impression in reading her works that Thérèse was in continual prayer. Like her spiritual Mother, the great St Teresa of Avila, from whom she may have learned it, she had the habit of breaking into prayer as she wrote. But these prayer asides are not artificial or contrived; they arise out of the topic that she is addressing.

Conclusion

It is clear that the foundations for Thérèse's vocation are to be found in her home. There is indeed progression and development when she enters Carmel, but her prayer in Carmel is somehow a seamless whole with her youth. It is the same God, the same Thérèse, and the same love that flowers into holiness in Carmel.

3

A Carmelite at Prayer

It should hardly be necessary to recall that St Thérèse of Lisieux was a Carmelite: the statues found in almost every church show her in the distinctive brown habit and white cloak of the Order. She was, moreover, a Discalced Carmelite, a point that still leads to some confusion and merits a few words of explanation.

Carmelites as we know them were to be found on the mountain range in the Holy Land called Mount Carmel from about the 1180s. They were hermits, many probably ex-crusaders, who lived in huts, called cells, along the mountainside. Early in the next century, these hermits approached the local bishop, St Albert, the Patriarch of Jerusalem, for a formula of life, which was afterwards called the Carmelite *Rule*. Saracen persecutions soon broke out and the hermits came to Europe where they found it impossible to live as they had done on Mount Carmel. In 1247 Pope Innocent IV approved adaptations of the *Rule*. By 1290 all the Carmelites had left Mount Carmel and the hermit brothers of Mount Carmel became numbered among the medieval friars. In the fourteenth-century, Carmelite nuns appeared, first in Italy and soon afterwards in Spain.

By the sixteenth century, the Carmelite Order, like many others, was in need of reform. In Spain, St Teresa of Avila (1515–1582) initiated a great reform, and after her death a reformed group of friars and nuns constituted the Discalced Carmelites (literally 'without shoes' and with the initials O.D.C). The parent Order, formally called the Ancient Observance, or more simply Carmelites (O.Carm.), somewhat later also had a reform, one centred in the Low Countries.

For a proper understanding of the prayer of Thérèse, we need to remember that she was both a Carmelite and belonged to the Discalced branch of the Order.

Carmelite

The original life on Mount Carmel was a contemplative one, most probably with very little pastoral or apostolic outreach. The *Rule* of Albert, even as mitigated by the popes, always retained a contemplative focus, even though in Europe this was no longer exclusive. When they became friars, the Carmelite brothers were engaged in service of the people. The women of Carmel kept a greater emphasis on the contemplative aspect.

As the order settled in Europe, certain values came to the fore. Carmelites never forgot their roots on Mount Carmel, the holy place sanctified by the prophet Elijah (see 1 Kgs 18). Indeed they looked to him as their spiritual father. The hermits had a chapel on Mount Carmel dedicated to St Mary, and in Europe they became known as the 'Brothers of the Blessed Virgin Mary of Mount Carmel'. There were two key symbols in early Carmelite writing: the desert, which featured so strongly in the life of Elijah (see 1 Kings 19:4–8) and the idea of being totally open to God (*vacare Deo*, empty for God). Both are connected: for the Carmelites the desert conjures up the idea not only of solitude, of being in communion with God, like Elijah, but also of being poor and free from all unnecessary goods or attachments. The significance of the desert is that it is the means or the place in which God is encountered and God is known as the supreme, indeed the only love.

In the writings of Thérèse we see these four themes: Mary, Elijah, the desert, and being empty for God. Firstly, we can note that, although she does not mention the prophet Elijah very frequently, the references are very important. Her cell was on the St Elijah corridor. She describes her reception of the Holy Spirit at confirmation in terms not of the great wind experienced by Elijah, but of the gentle breeze in which the Lord spoke to him (1 Kings 19:12–13); her profession too was marked by the same gentle breeze.[1] The words spoken by Elijah to God at that encounter form the Carmelite motto: 'I have been filled with a great zeal for the Lord God of hosts' (1 Kgs 19:10,14); it was frequently echoed by her, especially in the name, 'God of hosts' *(Dieu des armées)*. On two occasions she prays in the words of Elisha to his master Elijah, 'let me inherit a double share of your spirit' (2 Kgs 2:9),[2] and asks that her nothingness be transformed by fire, an allusion to the miracle of Elijah (1 Kgs 18:38).[3] Thus Thérèse takes up a theme then common in Catholic circles, namely the evil of the times, and tells her aunt about a sermon preached in the convent chapel on the feast of Our Lady of Mount Carmel:

> After having shown us the illustrious origins of our Holy Order, after having compared us to the Prophet Elijah fighting against the priests of Baal (1 Kgs 18:20–40), he declared: 'Times similar to those of Achab's persecution are about to begin again.' We seemed already to be flying to martyrdom.[4]

We note in the last reference the idea of Carmel inspired by the example of Elijah being deeply involved in the struggles of the Church.

The second Carmelite theme is the figure and person of Mary, known in the Order as the Mother and Beauty of Carmel. Mary is quite central in the life and writings of Thérèse, and there are many excellent studies on their relationship.[5] There are well over two hundred references to Mary or the Mother of God in Thérèse's writings. She was cured through the smile of Our Lady's statue from the psychosomatic illness that nearly killed her when she was ten. This strange illness was marked by hallucinations, both rigidity and uncontrolled body movements, weakness and a form of anorexia.[6] She received special graces at the shrine of Our Lady of Victories in Paris;[7] she composed a fine poem that she said summed up all she wanted to say about the Blessed Virgin, 'Why I love you O Mary'.[8] She stated that she would like to be a priest so that she could preach one sermon on Mary, showing her to be ordinary and rooted in the reality of life.[9] She referred to Pauline being clothed in Mary's garment and Céline adorned by Mary for her profession.[10] On the coat of arms she created for herself and Jesus, she recalled being clothed with the Carmelite habit as one of the great graces of her life.[11] On the day Thérèse died she constantly thought of and invoked the Virgin Mary.[12]

Thirdly, we note her handling of the Carmelite symbol of the desert. She uses it in two ways. She frequently speaks of life as a desert: 'Life [. . .] is a desert and an exile.'[13] In the playlet that she wrote, 'The Flight into Egypt', she enters into the natural beauty and threat of the desert.[14] But above all, Carmel is a desert. She says about her first evening in the convent, 'Everything thrilled me; I felt as though I was transported into a desert.'[15] In her *Story of a Soul*, the first part of which was addressed to Pauline, Thérèse later recalled her feelings at nine years of age when Pauline tried to explain her own vocation:

> When thinking over all you had said, I felt that Carmel was the *desert* where God wanted me to go and hide myself. I felt this with so much force that there wasn't the least doubt in my heart.[16]

Indeed, Thérèse had had an earlier childhood desire in which she was a hermit with Pauline in a desert.[17]

Fourthly, we note that Thérèse does not seem to have used the traditional Carmelite phrase, 'to be empty for God'. There was, however, a phrase that had been current in French spirituality for some two centuries, 'God alone' *(Dieu seul)*. This is found occasionally in her writings, but it would be difficult to know if it is an echo of this theme or a coincidental use of language.[18] But she certainly lived according to the spirit of both phrases, 'empty for God' and 'God alone', often expressed in her own characteristic language. It is perhaps most often found in the form of loving God or Jesus only or totally, and combined with the idea of her littleness. Thus reflecting on what she perceived as the vanities enjoyed by her young school-friends, she later wrote:

> I see that all is vanity and vexation of spirit under the sun [see Qoh 2:11], that the only good is to love God with all one's heart and to be poor in spirit here on earth.[19]

Or again, speaking of her First Communion she said that she developed a love for suffering, and 'I also felt the desire of loving only God, of finding my joy only in him.'[20] Even stronger was her sense of God loving her 'with a love of unspeakable foresight in order that I may now love him unto folly.'[21] A favourite word of Thérèse's was 'folly'; she uses it twenty-nine times in her writings, almost always with a significant weight of meaning. She speaks several times of loving unto folly, and of God's love and her own love being expressed in follies. The Carmelite theme of being empty for God thus finds in Thérèse a positive expression as total love for him.

These four core themes of Carmelite spirituality – Elijah and Mary, the desert, and being empty for God – were profoundly lived by Thérèse. Indeed, they are so much part of the Carmelite psyche that we can be sensitive to their presence even when they are not explicitly mentioned by a writer of the Order. But there are various ways in which these are lived in various branches of the Carmelite Family. They are also implied in the traditional language about the active and contemplative emphases of Carmelite life. But the reality is not quite as straightforward.

Active and contemplative

On their holy mountain, the early Carmelites were mainly contemplative. They may have given some limited service to the local Church, but we cannot be sure. There was a tradition going back at least to the time of St Anthony of Egypt (d. 356) for monks and hermits to be approached for spiritual direction. As we have seen, the hermits were forced to emigrate to Europe, where in time they became mendicant friars, engaged particularly in preaching and confessions work and having a special love of the scriptures. But though they were active, there was always nostalgia for Mount Carmel, with at times possibly a touch of schizophrenia, with Carmelites feeling torn between their ministry in the towns and an attraction for life as it was on Mount Carmel. The contemplative ideal has always been treasured in every part of the Carmelite Family. But even when the women's branch was founded, there was always a sense of contemplation being at the service of the Church. The greatest saints of Carmel like Teresa of Avila, Mary Magdalene de'Pazzi (d. 1607) and Thérèse herself were never inward-looking but alert to the deepest needs of the Church. Indeed, far from being exclusively devoted to prayer, these Carmelite saints saw themselves and their vocation as reflecting that of both Martha and Mary (see Luke 10:38–42).

The Carmelite *Rule:* the cell and silence

The Carmelite *Rule* has always been regularly read in the Order, especially in the early stages of religious life, called the novitiate. Thérèse refers to the 'Carmelite Rule' several times, but occasionally she means the Carmelite way of life, the Constitutions, local rules and customs, as when she says that the Carmelite rule does not permit correspondence during Advent.[22]

We shall encounter the *Rule* in various parts of this study. For the moment we would note only two of its special features. Firstly, the heart of the Carmelite *Rule* was traditionally considered to be chapter seven (now number 10):

> Each of you is to stay in his own cell or nearby, pondering the Lord's law day and night and keeping watch in his prayers unless attending to some other duty.

The exception 'unless attending . . .' covers work, attendance at Mass and other community exercises. To ponder the Lord's law is a traditional reference to reflecting on the Scriptures; it may echo the Vulgate or Latin text of Psalm 1:2 – delight in the law of the Lord, meditating on it day and night. In a later chapter we shall examine Thérèse's use of the Scriptures. She loved the small room, called the 'cell', assigned to her. Her joy in it is evident from her writings, and seems clearly to echo the *Rule*.[23] The cell itself was austere, indeed Thérèse referred to her sister Céline's 'poor little cell'.[24] It was 3.10 by 2.65 metres (about 10 x 8½ feet). It had no running water, electricity nor heating of any kind. She had an oil lamp and a bed (a straw mattress on two planks and trestles). In the cell there was a small bench seat, but neither table nor chair. She had a writing-case, which she would have placed on her knees. When not in use it lay on one of two rustic shelves. The simplicity of this cell was itself a reflection of the desert theme that we have seen as significant in Carmel. The cell was a place of prayer, quiet, study, reflection and rest.

Another important feature of the *Rule* was a long chapter on Silence (chapter 16, now number 21). Strict silence was prescribed from Compline (night prayer) until after Prime, the second liturgical prayer of the morning. Since it may not be very accessible, the chapter is worth quoting in full:

> The Apostle would have us keep silence, for in silence he tells us to work. As the Prophet also makes known to us: Silence is the way to foster holiness. Elsewhere he says: Your strength will lie in silence and hope. For this reason I lay down that you are to keep silence from after Compline until after Prime next day. At other times although you need not keep silence so strictly, be careful not to indulge in a great deal of talk, for as Scripture has it – and experience teaches us no less – Sin will not be wanting where there is much talk, and he who is careless in speech will come to harm; and elsewhere: The use of many words brings harm to the speaker's soul. And our Lord says in the Gospel: Every rash word uttered will have to be accounted for on judgement day. Make a balance then, each of you, to weigh his words in; keep a tight rein on your mouths, lest you stumble and fall in speech, and your fall be irreparable and prove mortal. Like the Prophet, watch your step lest your tongue give offence, and employ every care in keeping silent, which is the way to foster holiness.

These stipulations of the *Rule* were considered to be quite sufficient by Teresa of Avila, who adds very little about silence in her *Constitutions*, which in a religious order are more detailed, practical and time-conditioned laws or rules. Teresa mainly adds what is in fact a short interpretation of the words, 'you need not keep silence so strictly'. She says in her *Constitutions:* 'This rule of silence should not be understood to refer to a question and answer, or to a few words, for such things can be spoken without permission.'[25]

The origins of this silence in monastic and religious life were both practical – not to disturb the sleep or prayer of others – as well as spiritual. The *Rule* notes that sin can come about very easily through injudicious talk. But silence has also a positive value: the *Rule* calls silence 'the way to foster holiness' and states, alluding to Isaiah 30:15 'your strength will lie in silence and hope'. Thus silence has both negative and positive values. It is an ascetical exercise that has the added bonus of reducing sin that might arise through speech; it is the environment in which the Carmelite spirit finds expression.[26]

We find a subtle treatment of silence in Thérèse's writings, one that is relevant for her prayer and ours. There are occasional references in Thérèse's letters to times of silence: she writes letters in the time of silence; occasionally she transcribes during the silent time poetry that she has composed in her head during the day.[27] A few times she directly echoes the practical advice of the *Rule* as when she says, 'Take silence for example, what good it does to the soul, what failures to charity it prevents, and so many other troubles of all kinds. I speak especially about silence because it's on this point that we fail the most.'[28] A feature of Thérèse's asceticism was her habit of not defending herself, even when blamed in the wrong. She sees a model for this in Mary who did not defend herself to Martha (see Luke 10:38–42): 'She preferred to remain silent. O blessed silence that gives so much peace to souls.'[29]

In her later writings, which belong to the final eighteen months of her life, after she has entered into her profound trial of faith, Thérèse speaks several times both of the darkness and of the silence of our earthly exile.[30] There is a profound notion of silence, which is much more than the avoidance of speech or noise. Silence for Thérèse is a sacred space where she listens and where she meets her God. She treasures especially the holy silence of Advent and Lent.[31] In a letter to Céline there is an unattributed quotation, not yet traced by scholars: 'Virginity is a profound silence from all cares of this earth.'[32] Silence here resembles the other great Carmelite theme of the desert, in which we present an emptiness that God fills. In 1887 Mother Agnes had painted on the entrance to the corridor where Thérèse had her cell the words: 'Silence is the language of angels.' Thérèse uses it in a poem on mutual love which is headed by John 15:12 and begins:

> Silence is the sweet language
> Of the angels and all the elect.

> It must also be the lot
> Of souls who love each other in Jesus.[33]

Thérèse wrote in a letter to her sister Léonie, 'Silence is the language of the blessed inhabitants of heaven.'[34] Silence in such texts has almost the same value for Thérèse as the desert.

There are some other very important passages in which she speaks of the silence of Jesus. At times she looks to his silence at various times of his life or in the very Incarnation itself. Thus writing to Céline, who at the time was herself oscillating between consolation and aridity, Thérèse recalls that people were carried away with enthusiasm when the Lord spoke, 'He was trying to make them strong for the day of trial. . . . But how small the number of Our Lord's friends when he was silent before his judges! . . . Oh! what a melody for my heart is this silence of Jesus.'[35] In a poem, again for Céline who was finding the novitiate difficult, Thérèse wrote:

> This silence [of Jesus] is the first pledge
> Of his inexpressible love.
> Understanding this silent language,
> You will imitate him day by day.[36]

The silence of the Incarnation was a deep mystery:

> Word-God, remember that strange mystery.
> You kept silent and made an angel speak.[37]

Allied to these considerations are her deep intuitions into the silence of Mary. In her great poem 'Why I love you, O Mary!' she says of Mary:

> Oh Mary! How I love your eloquent silence!
> For me it is a sweet, melodious concert
> That speaks to me of the greatness and the power
> Of a soul that looks only to Heaven for help.

Later in the same poem she ponders the reticence of the Gospels about Mary after Calvary:

> Saint John's home becomes your only refuge.
> Zebedee's son is to replace Jesus . . . . .
> That is the last detail the Gospel gives.
> It tells me nothing more of the Queen of Heaven.
> But, O my dear Mother, doesn't its profound silence
> Reveal that the Eternal Word Himself
> Wants to sing the secrets of your life
> To charm your children, all the Elect of Heaven.[38]

There is also a most important theme of the silence of Jesus who leaves her or Céline in aridity: 'Jesus is sleeping and the angel remains in his mysterious silence.'[39] She wrote to her sister, Pauline, who was now Mother Agnes, about her retreat: 'Nothing near Jesus. Aridity! . . . Sleep! But at least there is silence . . . Silence does good to the soul.'[40] Again, she writes a poem for a cousin whose prayer for a baby was apparently being unanswered:

> But, Lord, you make me understand
> Your mysterious silence.
> Yes you tell me by your silence:
> 'Your sighs go right up to heaven.'[41]

Like her beloved St John of the Cross, who pondered on 'Silent music, sounding solitude,'[42] she delights in the communication of Jesus in and through silence: 'this Beloved instructs my soul, He speaks to it in silence.'[43] Her prayer too is sometimes silence for she writes in an affectionate letter to her aunt, Madame Guérin: 'Frequently only silence can express my prayer, however, this divine Guest of the tabernacle understands all, even the silence of a child's soul filled with gratitude.'[44] In a poem for her cousin Marie, who is entering the Lisieux Carmel, she has Marie say about her new Carmelite vocation:

From now on, near the Eucharist, I shall be able
To sacrifice myself in silence, to wait for heaven in peace.[45]

It remains for us to see how this value of silence is integrated into her prayer. At this point we can raise the point of the ongoing relevance of silence for the prayer of each one of us. We can all certainly take on board the need for some, perhaps greater, silence in our lives. Most of us talk too much, and our speech is not always an example of gospel charity. Worse still, we can often be silent when we should speak, or we voice what would best be left unsaid. The Carmelite *Rule* has wise words on silence as a way of avoiding sin that we can still ponder. More significantly it has advice for many of us who are surrounded by too much noise, not only the noise that can be measured in decibels, but the noise of distractions, anxieties, cares and shallow entertainment. Even secular business gurus advocate a time of quiet in which busy executives can relax, meditate, get in contact with their feelings and put things in perspective. But there are other values, which we find especially emphasised within the Discalced Carmelite tradition.

A Discalced Carmelite

We have seen that the discalced branch of the Carmelite Order owes its origins to the reforms in Spain of Teresa of Avila. As a result, it is much more focussed than the parent Order. The Discalced Order had a founder, St Teresa of Avila, along with her disciple, St John of the Cross; the original Order appeared on Mount Carmel with no known founders. Among the Discalced, Teresa is often referred to as 'our holy Mother' (in Spanish *La Madre*) and her works are quite central to Discalced spirituality and formation. In the other main branch of the Carmelite Order, St Teresa of Avila is just one of the many great spiritual authors and saints, perhaps indeed even the greatest. In France, men and women from both the Ancient and Discalced branches suffered a terrible toll during the French Revolution. Even by the time of Thérèse, the Order had not recovered. The nuns suffered some isolation in particular, the discalced friars did not have a very great influence on them. The latter's ecclesiastical superiors were more often bishops and their nominees, rather than the provincial superior of the friars.

Formation at the time of Thérèse was largely done through reading the Carmelite *Rule* and the key writings of the holy Mother, St Teresa. It also consisted in the passing on of an oral tradition, which was handed down through generations in the convents and shared with other Carmels especially through the circulars or obituary notes that were sent around to other Carmels after the death of a sister. Except where we have obvious allusions to the Carmelite *Rule* or to its saints, mainly Teresa and John, it is not easy to identify the origins of the precise Carmelite contours of the Lisieux Carmel and of Thérèse. Suffice to say that though she is unique and very creative within her tradition, she is instantly recognisable as a Carmelite. Her prayer, which we now begin to examine in detail, is no less unique and Carmelite.

4

Liturgical Prayer

When we come to examine the prayer of Thérèse, we see that it consisted of three major elements: the Divine Office (which, since Vatican II, we have learned to call 'The Prayer of the Church'); daily Mass; and mental prayer. In addition there were various vocal prayers, in particular the Rosary, which she said daily. We deal with each of these in the following four chapters, beginning with the Office.

The saying of the Office occupied a substantial part of the Carmelite's day – about three hours. This prayer was said from the breviary and consisted of psalms, scriptural and other readings, hymns and prayers. The word 'breviary' (Latin, *breviarium*) probably meant originally a short conspectus or collection of the offices. In time it became a substantial work, comprising four volumes, one for each season of the year, spring, summer, autumn, winter.

Origins of the Office

The Office evolved over a long period during which it became ever more complex. The idea of prayer at fixed hours was common among the Jews and was taken over by the early Church. Thus we find Peter and John going up to the temple at the hour of prayer (see Acts 3:1). An important book on Church life, which appeared in Syria about AD 95, *The Didachê*, recommended the recitation of the *Our Father* three times daily – other prayers were undoubtedly added. During the next and following century the custom grew of praying at night and in the morning, as well as at the third, sixth and ninth hours. Soon the idea arose that the morning and evening prayer was obligatory.

When we come to the first monks, called the 'Desert Fathers' ('Mothers' came later), there was a concern to fulfil the command of

scripture: 'Pray without ceasing' (1 Thess 5:17). Some groups of
monks took the phrase so literally that different parties of monks
took over from one another in saying the psalms, so that in an area
there was always prayer. By the time of the Benedictine monks in the
West, the Office was divided into eight parts, later to be called
'hours'. These evolved significantly throughout the centuries. As part
of the evolution, the contact with the original time for saying the
hours was lost, so that they were generally said earlier than their name
would indicate. Thus Vespers or Evening prayer was said in the
middle of the day. (Older readers may recall that the Easter Vigil
celebrations before 1954 took place on the morning of Holy
Saturday.)

The hours of the Office

The Office consisted of eight hours, though some would preserve the
special number seven by combining two. There was Matins (Latin:
matutinus, 'of the morning'), an office of psalms and readings, often
said at night. The morning office was of Lauds (from Latin *laudate*,
'Praise', which was the opening word of many psalms used in it). It
consisted of four psalms, an Old Testament canticle, scripture
reading and the *Benedictus* (the song of Zechariah in Luke 1:68–79).
As this was linked with Matins said at night, another morning hour
was added, called 'Prime' (Latin *prima*, 'first' hour, about 6 a.m.)
which consisted of a hymn, psalms, scripture lesson or reading,
prayers for various needs, and in the middle was the proclamation of
the *Martyrology*. This was a book with a section for every day of the
year which commemorated the martyrs (hence the name) and saints
who died or were venerated on that day. The hours of Terce, Sext and
None were assigned to the third, sixth and ninth hours, that is 9.00
a.m., 12.00 noon and 3.00 p.m. In practice they were all said
together at 6.00 a.m. These had a hymn, short scripture reading and
three psalms. The evening office was Vespers (Latin: *vesper*, 'evening'):
this consisted of hymn, five psalms, reading and centrally the
Magnificat (Mary's hymn of praise, Luke 1:46–55). The night hour
was Compline (Latin: *Completorium*, indicating 'completion'), a
short office with psalms, hymn, reading and the canticle of Simeon,

Nunc dimmitis, Luke 2:29–32); this hour had night themes, especially vigilance and protection from evil.

Carmelites and the Office

The Carmelite *Rule* reflected the life on Mount Carmel. It envisaged two situations. Those who knew how to read were to recite the psalms in their solitary cells according to the customs of the local Church. Those who could not read were to say the prayer they knew, the *Our Father,* a specified number of times in place of each of the hours.

When the Carmelites came to Europe they were obliged to say the hours together like other friars and clerics:

> Those who know how to say the canonical hours with those in orders should do so, in the way those holy forefathers of ours laid down, and according to the Church's approved custom. Those who do not know the hours must say twenty-five 'Our Fathers' for the night office, except on Sundays and solemnities when that number is to be doubled so that the 'Our Father' is said fifty times; the same prayer must be said seven times in the morning in place of Lauds, and seven times too for each of the hours, except for Vespers when it is said fifteen times.[1]

A central feature of the mendicant or friars' way of life adopted by the Carmelites in Europe was that of praying with the people and for them. What was new to the Carmelites also was the choral recitation: the community divided in two saying alternately the verses of the psalms. The part of the church where Office was celebrated was called the 'choir'. Since medieval friars also travelled and undertook pastoral work, gradually the idea arose of saying privately what one did not say with the community.

By the time of St Teresa of Avila, the Office had become very elaborate. It was mostly sung, which meant that there was time for little else. Two important elements of the Carmelite life had more or less gone by the board – extended personal prayer and work. There were two keys to the reforms of Teresa, in addition to her emphasis on poverty. One was the enclosure, which, by cutting off contact with the outside world, protected the contemplative dimension of life. The second was largely the elimination of singing of the Offices, so that she freed up time for both work and personal prayer. She wrote in her *Constitutions:*

> The chant should never be sung with musical notation, but should be chanted in a monotone and with uniform voices. Ordinarily, everything should be recited, and also the Mass, for the Lord will be served if some time remains so that the Sisters may earn their livelihood.[2]

This chanted office still took several hours per day. It remained a central part of the prayer life of Carmel.

The Office at Lisieux

In Thérèse's time, the Office was spread throughout the day. But the time at which the parts were said no longer reflected the original meaning of each part. In winter the sisters rose at 5.45 a.m. and, after an hour of silent prayer, said all the small hours – Prime, Terce, Sext and None. Vespers were said at 2 p.m. and Compline at 7.40 p.m.. Matins and Lauds, which took between 75 and 100 minutes, were said at 9 p.m.. (In Summer the nuns rose an hour earlier, and everything was advanced by sixty minutes to allow for a siesta or rest period at 1 p.m.)

The Divine Office at Lisieux was said in Latin. It was customary however to have a translation of the Matins texts read in the refectory. Since Thérèse did not understand Latin, one can wonder what the Office meant to her.

Our idea of the Office, or The Liturgy of the Hours, is largely conditioned by our experience of its post-Vatican II reforms. The Council devoted a special chapter of the liturgy document to it. The main points were the following:

• The Office is a share in the priestly work of Christ.
• It is a praise of the Lord and intercession for the salvation of the world.

- It is a prayer of Christ the Head with his Body, the Church.
- It brings us to stand before God's throne in the name of the Church.
- It enables us to fulfil the exhortation of St Paul, 'Pray without ceasing' (1 Thess 5:17).
- It makes the day holy.
- It is, as the public prayer of the Church, a source of piety and of nourishment for personal prayer.
- It is the voice of the Church, of the whole Mystical Body, publicly praising God.[3]

The introduction printed in reformed Office books (called *General Instruction*) develops a rich theology and spirituality of the Liturgy of the Hours. The prime mover of the liturgical reforms stemming from Vatican II, Archbishop H. Bugnini, has noted that this introduction is 'one of the most important, if not the most outstanding of the entire post-Conciliar liturgical reform'.[4]

St Thérèse and the Office

We can wonder how much of this modern understanding was available to Thérèse or might be found reflected in her writings. We might begin by thinking about the title commonly given to the Office in Benedictine circles, the *Opus Dei*. This 'work of God' has two senses – it is a work belonging to God or offered in praise; it is also God's work in us, which enables us to offer praise. The person praying the psalms is returning to God the inspired word, making a prayer whose acceptability is almost guaranteed.

Since the Office was so central in Carmel we should not expect very many references to it: being so much part of daily life it was taken for granted. Thérèse's family had always attended Vespers on Sundays. She remarks that her mother had stayed at home with her when she 'was too little to go to the services'[5] (*offices*, which comprised of morning Mass and in the evening Vespers, Compline and Benediction). Later she recalled her melancholy thoughts at the time of Compline each Sunday: the day of repose was ending and soon ordinary tasks would return.[6] One of the highlights of her pre-

First Communion retreat in the Benedictine Abbey was going with the religious to recite all the Divine Office.[7]

The most significant reference to the Office in Thérèse's writings is from the last months of her life. Speaking of her difficulty in finding vocal prayers that suited her, she makes an exception for the Office, saying,

> Outside the *Divine Office* which I am *very unworthy* to recite, I do not have the courage to force myself to search out *beautiful* prayers in books.[8]

In this single sentence, Thérèse underlined 'Divine Office', 'very unworthy' and 'beautiful'. One wonders what concept of the Office lay behind the aside about her unworthiness to recite it. One might immediately suspect the influence of Fr Godefroid Madelaine, a Premonstratensian who had preached retreats in the Carmel in 1882, 1890 and 1896. He was a competent theologian to whom the Carmel later committed the revision of *The Story of a Soul.* Moreover, he belonged to an order that set a high store on liturgical prayer. We also know that by the nineteenth century, Benedictine circles had embraced the idea of the Office being the Prayer of the Church or of its being said for the Church; we might readily assume that some sense of the dignity of the Office would have been communicated to Thérèse by the Benedictine sisters with whom we know she discussed prayer as a child. We have already alluded to the reading of Guéranger's *The Liturgical Year* in her home; it was also read in the convent refectory. This had a fine sense of the Office being a prayer of the Church for the Church, one united with the continuous intercession of Jesus, the High Priest (see Heb 7:24–25). But there are other indications about what Thérèse may have meant, and about how she understood the Office.

For her sister Céline's profession, Thérèse wrote her a letter in which she composed a highly imaginative account of how the court of heaven would enjoy the celebration. Nowadays one might think of the phrase, 'over the top', but we know that Céline had a taste for elaborate embellishment and Thérèse here indulged her. The letter is also important evidence of how Thérèse understood many aspects of Carmelite life. Towards the end she thinks of their parents being present and adds:

> I forgot, too, to express the joy of Jesus when He hears Céline pronounce for the first time the words of the Office, which will be her task, the spouse of His Heart being entrusted with charming him in the midst of the camps.[9]

A certain knowledge of Carmelite customs is necessary to grasp the meaning of this postscript. At each celebration one sister presides at the Office, that is, begins it with the words, 'O Lord come to my aid', says the main prayer of the Office, and gives the blessings that precede each reading. Usually sisters were in turn assigned this task for a week; the name for her office was 'hebdomadarian' (Greek: *hebdomados*, 'week'). At the Lisieux Carmel it was customary for a sister to preside at the Office for the first time on her profession day. It would not be the first time she joined in recitation of the Office, but from that day on, there was a more serious obligation to attend. Thérèse is referring to this custom. Reciting the Office is, Thérèse says, like 'a choir of music in the army camp'. This is a favourite text of Thérèse taken from a rather poor translation of the Song of Songs 7:1. She had already given a long explanation of the text to Céline about two years earlier. She then used the text to indicate that our lives in earthly exile are a song to please Jesus.[10] Here we see Thérèse expressing the idea that the Office is a way of giving pleasure, that is praise, to God or Jesus.

In one of her most elaborate poems, 'Jesus, my Beloved, Remember' she meditates on the life of Jesus. In recalling his nights of prayer, she writes:

> Remember that you would often climb
> The hills at sunset.
> Remember your divine prayers,
> Your love songs at the hour of sleep.
> O my God, I offer your prayers with delight.
> During my hours of prayer, and then at the Divine Office,

There so close to your Heart,
I sing with joy:
Remember.[11]

Here the Divine Office is a prayer in union with Jesus' own prayer.
Thérèse's global thought about and especially her feeling for the
Office is not far from the rich exposition of Vatican II, though it
lacks the latter's technical theological language:

> Jesus Christ, high priest of the new and eternal covenant,
> taking human nature, introduced into this earthly exile that
> hymn which is sung throughout all ages in the realms above.
> He joins the entire community of humankind to himself,
> associating it with himself in singing his divine song of praise.[12]

The Office is a reflection of Christ's prayer before his Father, which
began on earth and continues in heaven (see Heb 7:25 with
4:16–5:1).

There are several significant references to the Office from the last
months of her life. At this time she was confined to bed and unable
to be physically present with the sisters in choir. She regretted this
and wondered if she would not have been better to have concealed
her illness more. She says that she had prayed that God would allow
her to join in the community acts right up to her death.[13] Being
deprived of Holy Communion and of the Divine Office was a special
hardship of her illness.[14] She noted the pleasure of being able to see
the stars and to hear the Office through an open window.[15] The
following is an important comment on the Office in her reflections
about seven weeks before she died:

> How proud I was when I was hebdomadarian during the
> recitation of the Divine Office, reciting the prayers out loud in
> the centre of the Choir! I was proud because I remembered
> that the priest said the same prayers during Mass, and I had the
> right, like him, to pray aloud before the Blessed Sacrament,
> giving the blessings and the absolutions, reading the Gospel
> when I was first chantress.

However, I must also admit that this Office was at once my happiness and my martyrdom. I had a great desire to recite it well, without making any mistakes. Sometimes, even after being aware only a minute before of what I was supposed to say, I would let it pass without opening my mouth because of a totally involuntary distraction. I don't believe that one could have a greater desire to recite the Office more perfectly than I and to be present in Choir. I excuse very much those Sisters who forget or make mistakes during the Office.[16]

There are several points to be made about this complex text. She refers to the priest saying the same prayer as at Mass; the central prayer of the Mass and of the Office is the same. Secondly, this text is another one in which Thérèse may express some desire for priesthood, though its significance should not be exaggerated.[17] We know that Thérèse had a very high esteem for the priesthood. She mentions prayer for priests, which was her special Carmelite vocation, over a dozen times in her writings. Her family held priests in high esteem, so much so that the rather worldly behaviour of some of the priests on the pilgrimage to Rome of Thérèse, her father and Céline was a source of some scandal. In a poem written for a sacristan at Carmel, Thérèse reflects on the priestly dimension of the office of sacristan:

> Sublime mission of the Priest,
> You become our mission here below.
> Transformed by the Divine Master,
> It is he who guides our steps.
> We must help the apostles
> By our prayers, our love.
> Their battlefields are ours
> For them we fight each day.[18]

In a letter to Céline four years earlier she reflected on the dignity of the office of prayer, and remarked, 'I find our share is really beautiful, what have we to envy in priests?'[19] Yet it is easy to understand her pleasure in praying in the Church and for the Church using the same words as the priest at Mass. She was very conscious of the imperfect way in which she said the Office. Her biggest problem was distractions, a problem that she also had with the Rosary as we shall see later. She could not understand the Latin texts she was reading. Therefore, though she entered the Office with a general sense of what the prayer was, the words themselves could not hold her attention. And this was her situation for about three hours each day. Nevertheless she loved the Office, as her reflection especially from her last months have made clear to us. Another point we should note is that in Thérèse's day the Office was very complex: there were special rubrics about bowing, genuflecting, standing, sitting, and kneeling. The text was not straightforward: there were psalms and other parts of the Office to be got from different places in the Breviary. It required a lot of concentration. Moreover, correct and exact observance of the rubrics was seen as a way of offering God homage; there could be no carelessness or sloppiness in divine worship. For many religious and priests the saying of the Office became a burden with anxiety or scrupulosity attached to the correct way of saying it. Thérèse is quite free from this latter. Even though she regrets her mistakes, she is ready to excuse them in others and, one suspects, in herself. The Office is a matter of love and worship rather than a juridical obligation.

If one asks about any other source of Thérèse's special love of the Office, one can point to the spirituality of the time, which set high store by the Office. But in particular one should not neglect St Teresa of Avila, who clearly loved the Office and received many of her mystical graces during it. There were several pages of penal legislation added to Teresa's *Constitutions*, which were almost certainly not of her composition. Such legislation was common in religious institutes of the time. They included several penalties for carelessness or faults committed in the recitation of the Office – coming late, being unprepared, making mistakes in ceremonial, singing in unapproved fashion, etc.[20] It is not easy to know if these punishments were in force in Thérèse's time. But she is clearly conscious of the need to avoid mistakes, even though the text we have quoted indicates that she would have been indulgent towards those who make mistakes.

Her sister Céline has recorded some other interesting references to the Office as seen by Thérèse. As assistant Novice-Mistress Thérèse did not want any amusing or distracting thought to be communicated before the Office.[21] One knows that spending long hours saying an Office in an unknown language left the novices sufficiently prone to distraction.

Céline also gives us a glimpse of her sister's way of reciting the Office:

> Thérèse's whole bearing in choir was one of great modesty and recollection. In this she was an inspiration to us all. I asked her one day about her interior dispositions in choir and she replied that she had no fixed method of prayer at that time. She went on to say that often she transported herself in spirit, during the Office, to some desert-cliff high above this earth. There alone with Jesus, with the world at her feet, she would forget that creatures existed, and would simply tell Him over and over again how much she loved Him. True she did not always understand the language she was using to express her love, but she added, it was enough for her to realise that she was making Him happy.[22]

At the process for beatification, Céline testified to Thérèse's love for the Office:

> At Carmel, the Servant of God [Thérèse] had a special attraction for the recitation of the liturgical office. [. . .] She taught us to be careful of our exterior disposition during the Office on account of the dignity of the task we were fulfilling.[23]

Céline recounts also Thérèse's special joy at hearing the names of the saints at Prime:

> She told me that after she had asked the inhabitants of heaven to adopt her as their child, she used to listen each morning with special reverence and devotion to the Martyrology at

Prime when the roll-call of her 'close relatives up there' was
read aloud in choir.[24]

Thérèse's awareness of the Communion of Saints is a major theme in
all her writing.[25]

The psalms

The greater part of the Divine Office is made up of the psalms.
Thérèse had a special love for them. Of the four hundred references
to the Old Testament in her writings, nearly half are to texts of the
psalms, by way of allusion, citation or extended reflection.[26] We know
that she studied the psalms carefully. In the beatification process Sr
Marie de la Trinité stated:

> She [Thérèse] said to me another time: 'At the Office of Sext,
> there is a verse which I pronounce always reluctantly *(à contre-
> coeur)*. It is this: *Inclinavi cor meum ad faciendas justificationes
> tuas in aeternum propter retributionem* (I have inclined my
> heart to do thy justifications for ever for the reward). Within
> me I am eager to say *(je m'empresse de dire):* "Oh my Jesus, you
> know well that it is not for the reward that I serve you, but
> only because I love you, and to save souls".'[27]

Here we have evidence that Thérèse not only sought the meaning of
the Latin text, but she brought together a French translation and the
Latin Office book or Breviary. In this text also we see Thérèse's
motivation for her life and also for her liturgical prayer: love of Jesus
and the salvation of souls.

Lessons for today

We have come a long way from the pre-Vatican II view of the Divine
Office, which for many priests had become not the *opus Dei* (the
work of God), but *onus diei* (the daily burden). The moral books of
the time taught that the omission of a single hour of the Office (less
than five minutes in private celebration) constituted a mortal sin.
The Office was so surrounded by anxiety and scrupulosity that Pope
Leo X attached a special indulgence to the prayer *Sacrosanctae:* it took

away guilt and temporal punishment arising from human frailty in the recitation of the Office.[28]

For Thérèse, the Office was a task willingly undertaken in love. It was an act of adoration that she saw as pleasing Jesus. But she saw the Office as more than her prayer to the Lord. There is also some ecclesial sense: she was in some way united to priests who celebrated the Office and also said at Mass the central prayer for each hour. She was also clearly aware that it was the prayer of the Church.

Thérèse did not have all the insights of the post-Vatican II Church that we noted earlier in this chapter. But she does indicate some essential aspects of the Office. It is divine worship, and not primarily something that we do for our satisfaction. There is objectivity about the Office, which is quite contrary to the individualism of many Christians today.

More significantly, she can remind all of us that the Liturgy of the Hours is above all a celebration of love and respect for God. It expresses not perhaps what we are but what we would like to be before the Lord. It is moreover one of the notable ways in which we can show a concern for others, pleading with and on behalf of the world.

Lastly, her struggles to say the Office well, despite the tedium of chanting in a language she did not understand, shows us that, in prayer, patient endurance is an essential virtue. It was in loving the Office and in loving through the Office that she served her God and her Church.

5

The Eucharist

The Eucharist was central to the spirituality of St Thérèse of Lisieux, even from her childhood. She did not live in a age when daily Communion was possible, though daily Mass was the norm in her family and at the Lisieux Carmel. Before looking at what she said about the Eucharist, it would be helpful to consider both her Carmelite background and the situation of the French Church at the time.

Carmelite *Rule* and practice

The hermits on Mount Carmel were given a rule or way of life by the local Patriarch, St Albert of Jerusalem, about 1208. In it he wrote:

> An oratory as conveniently as possible is to be built in the midst of the cells, where early in the morning you shall come together each day to hear Mass where this can be done without difficulty.[1]

There are several points to be noted about this brief text.[2] The cells of the hermits were scattered on the mountain range called Mount Carmel. Following the way of life proposed by Albert, there is to be a new centre for the whole group of hermits – the oratory. We can see this chapel not only as geographically central, but also as the spiritual heart of the community. Indeed, the permission from the bishop to have an oratory and to celebrate Mass was at the time the equivalent of ecclesiastical approbation for a group. Daily Mass was not unusual for religious at the time. The clause 'where this can be done without difficulty' is hard to interpret: it probably refers to having a priest available; it may also be an indication that serious difficulty for a hermit, such as weather conditions, would excuse attendance.

We should note that the injunction is to come together for Mass. Daily Communion was not common at the time. Indeed, the question of the frequency of Communion has had a complex history in the Church.[3] In the early Church, Communion would seem to have been weekly. A few centuries later, daily Communion was common in many places, but by the sixth century this practice had lapsed. In many places, by the time of the Carmelite Rule, Communion was received only several times a year, or at best monthly. The early *Constitutions* of the Carmelite Order specified that all members of the community communicate seven or eight times a year; these were solemn occasions when all the brethren received both the host and chalice. Apart from these special community occasions, they were also free to receive Communion on Sundays and on the greater feasts.[4] This legislation continued up to the Reformation, with Communion generally becoming more frequent. Some communities of nuns received more frequently or less frequently than these norms. We know that the Carmelite nun, St Mary Magdalene de' Pazzi (d. 1607) chose the convent at Florence precisely because, unusually for the time, it had the custom of daily Communion. Later the inroads of Jansenism would make Communion less frequent.

Nineteenth-Century France

Jansenism was a movement centred in France and in the Low Countries, which stemmed from a book, *Augustinus*, published two years after the death of its author, Cornelius Otto Jansen (d. 1638). His disciples were extremely rigorist about salvation, about divine and Church law, and about sin. As a movement Jansenism had died out in the early years of the nineteenth century, but its spirit lingered, especially with regard to Holy Communion. There were two Jansenist teachings that did enormous damage. The first was that the prime reason for the existence of the Blessed Sacrament was to honour the majesty of God and give homage to God as the First Principle. The sanctification of the faithful was only a secondary reason for its institution. St Thérèse is clearly reacting against such views in her famous saying:

It is not to remain in a golden ciborium that He comes down to us each day from heaven; it's to find another heaven, infinitely more dear to Him than the first: the heaven of our soul, made to his image, the living temple of the adorable Trinity.[5]

The second harmful Jansenist teaching held that for the reception of Holy Communion perfect contrition was required. If the conditions for perfection contrition were then to be narrowly presented, many people would be afraid to risk receiving the sacrament. Such teaching gave rise to many scruples.

There was opposition to these Jansenist teachings particularly from Jesuits and from St Alphonsus Liguori (d. 1787). The latter favoured frequent Communion, and taught that the confessor should determine the number of times a particular person could receive it. This view was to be very influential. Another anti-Jansenist thrust in the Church arose from the apparitions of the Sacred Heart to St Margaret Mary Alacoque (d. 1690). These apparitions favoured Holy Communion on the First Fridays, and the practice of the Holy Hour.

This double background, Carmelite and French, needs to be kept in mind as we consider St Thérèse's practice and thoughts about the Eucharist.[6] We know that daily Communion was not customary in the Lisieux Carmel. Permission for reception rested with the confessor and to an extent with the Carmelite superior. Thérèse recalled her special joy when, during an influenza epidemic that laid low most of the community, leaving only herself and two others on their feet, she was given permission over a short period to receive Communion daily.[7] This epidemic broke out just after Christmas in 1891. A year earlier the Vatican Congregation of Bishops and Religious had decreed that if the confessor allowed frequent, even daily Communion, the religious superior was not to interfere. Thérèse was delighted with this decree, and observed: 'The mother prioress should not determine the frequency of Communion. That always surprised me.'[8] However, the norms of the Holy See were not observed at Lisieux. Thérèse regretted very much the opposition of Mother de Gonzague. Her sister Marie recalled:

> She [Thérèse] said, a short time before her death to Mother Marie de Gonzague, who was afraid of daily Communion: "Mother, when I'm in heaven, I'll make you change your opinion." This is what happened. After the death of the Servant of God, the chaplain gave us Communion every day, and Mother Marie de Gonzague, instead of being repelled by it, was very happy about it.[9]

Soon it would no longer be an issue in the Church: in 1905 Pope Pius X issued a decree 'On Frequent Communion'.[10] The present legislation of the Church is 'that it is in keeping with the very meaning of the Eucharist that the faithful, if they have the required dispositions, receive communion each time they participate in the Mass.'[11] A person may even receive a second time, if they are present at Mass again the same day.[12]

First Communion

Her First Communion was one of the greatest moments of grace in Thérèse's whole life. She had already shared deeply in the preparations for Céline's big day and regretted that she could not receive Communion with her. Céline, four years older than Thérèse, made her First Communion in May 1880. We have already seen that Thérèse saw it as a great day in her own life.[13]

That same year Thérèse made her First Confession, but it would be four years more before she could receive Communion.

Thérèse was given three months of intensive preparation by Marie, who was her godmother and sister. It was very solid indeed. Marie, still at home in Les Buissonnets, encouraged her to make acts of love and to say aspirations, recording all of these in a notebook. Marie wrote her a letter each week that Thérèse later said gave her 'deep thoughts' and aided her 'in the practice of virtue'.[14] She recalled in particular four subjects on which Marie had given her instruction: life's struggles; the eternal riches that can be amassed each day; the way of becoming holy through fidelity in little things; renunciation. This last was a leaflet, and Thérèse said, 'I meditated upon this with delight.'[15] Seeing the maturity and depth of these themes, we have to remind ourselves that Thérèse was then only eleven years of age.

As an immediate preparation for First Communion the pupils went to the local Benedictine Abbey school for a three-day retreat, given by the chaplain Fr Amélie Domin. During this retreat Thérèse made her second confession. Her description of her First Communion is one of the finest pages of her entire works[16] and it can stand comparison with the writings of the great mystics:

> Ah! how sweet was that first kiss of Jesus! It was a kiss of *love*, I *felt* that I *was loved*, and I said: 'I love You, and I give myself to You forever!' There were no demands made, no struggles, no sacrifices; for a long time now Jesus and poor little Thérèse *looked at* and understood each other. That day, it was no longer a *look*, it was a fusion; they were no longer two, Thérèse had vanished as a drop of water is lost in the immensity of the ocean. Jesus alone remained; He was the Master, the King. Had not Thérèse asked Him to take away her *liberty*, for her *liberty* frightened her? She felt so feeble and fragile that she wanted to be united forever to the divine Strength! Her joy was too great, too deep for her to contain, and tears of consolation soon flowed.[17]

We notice here that in describing this intense moment of grace, Thérèse unusually uses the third person, speaking of 'Thérèse' rather than the customary, 'I'. Were we to make the substitution of 'I', the passage would feel quite different. As it is, Thérèse is almost standing back, objectively evaluating and marvelling at the grace she has been given. Her tears were misunderstood, and the onlookers thought that she missed her mother at that great moment. Instead she tells us she had a deep sense of the Communion of Saints, and of the presence of her mother along with the heaven that had entered her soul.[18] A possible key to this text, with its central imagery of ocean, is found in her autobiography, as she recalls the time about five years earlier when she first saw the sea. Looking at the trail of light over the sea at sunset, she remarked, 'And near Pauline, I made the resolution never to wander away from the glance of Jesus in order to travel peacefully towards the eternal shore.'[19]

Her First Communion was the occasion of other special graces. On the afternoon of the same day she made an Act of Consecration to the Blessed Virgin. She felt a special bond between herself and the Mother of God.[20] The following day began a time of a great desire to suffer, which was reinforced at her Confirmation about a month later. Thérèse's attitude to suffering is surprising at first sight and extremely complex. She matured in her approach and understanding throughout her life. At the deepest root of her attitude is not so much a desire for suffering as a value in itself, but as a way in which she can respond to the profound love overwhelming her at this time.[21] Having once received Communion, Thérèse was not slow to seek permission for more occasions. A notebook she kept tells us that she received Communion twenty-two times in the following sixteen months, which was quite frequent for the time.

She would soon find great distress in her love for the Eucharist. It was customary to celebrate First Communion in a solemn way about a year after the actual First Communion. Thérèse again went into retreat in preparation. Though it was the same retreat-master, Fr Domin, this time his negative talks on issues such as sin and punishment were the occasion of a profound crisis of scruples that would last from May 1885 to October 1886.[22]

The word 'scruples' has a range of meanings. In Thérèse's case it meant the acute anxiety about having committed sin, when in fact she had not. Serious scrupulosity, not to be confused with a sensitive conscience, is a most painful and destructive psychological illness. Thérèse herself speaks of 'a terrible sickness of scruples', which she called 'a martyrdom'. At the time of Thérèse, the only cure for it was to allow somebody else (usually a confessor) to determine if there was guilt, and to obey the other person completely, especially with regard to receiving Communion. Thérèse confided her scruples to Marie, who handled them with extraordinary sensitivity and skill. No one, not even her confessors, suspected her problem; indeed they gave her permission to receive Communion quite frequently. When her guide Marie told a distraught Thérèse that she, too, was entering Carmel, Thérèse turned in prayer to her brothers and sisters who had died in infancy, and she was immediately set free, through, she believed, their love and intercession. The experience of these eighteen months matured Thérèse so that a few years later she was to pen a remarkable letter on scruples and on the Eucharist.

A letter of Thérèse (LT 92)

In May 1889 Thérèse was a novice. She had been in the Lisieux Carmel a little over a year. Her cousin, three years her senior, Marie Guérin, had suffered from scrupulosity. Visiting the Paris Exhibition she was overly disturbed by what she saw there and in the city. She felt unable to receive Communion and wrote to Thérèse in distress.[23] The reply from Thérèse is one of the most interesting of all her early letters. She wrote to assure her cousin that she fully understands the temptation to desist from Communion, but regards it as a mistake. The advice she gave her cousin exactly mirrored what she had received from her sister, Marie, in her own crisis of scruples. Her insistence that she understood her cousin's state of mind is an indication that, though Thérèse seems not to have had serious struggles in the area of chastity, she nonetheless 'was not spared the confusion of scruples in this domain'.[24]

The major interest of this letter lies in its Eucharistic doctrine. When the vice postulator of the beatification of Thérèse asked Pius X to read this letter, the Pope said, 'This is most opportune. It is a great joy for me . . . . We must hurry this cause.'[25] What seems to have attracted Pius X was Thérèse's recommendation of frequent Communion well in advance of his own decree on the subject in 1905. We should also note some key points of her Eucharistic spirituality. She sees the loving heart as a more important tabernacle than the one on the altar. The devil, she says, has managed to put Marie off receiving the Lord:

> He wants to deprive Jesus of a loved tabernacle *(d'un tabernacle aimé)*, and not being able to enter this sanctuary, he wants at least, that it remain *empty* and without any Master! . . . And what will become of this poor heart? . . .When the devil has succeeded in drawing the soul away from Holy Communion, *he has won everything*. . . . And Jesus weeps. . . . Oh, my darling, think, then, that Jesus is there in the Tabernacle

expressly for *you*, for *you alone;* He is burning with the desire to enter your heart . . . so don't listen to the devil, mock him, and go without fear to receive Jesus in peace and love! . . .[26]

She goes on to reassure her cousin, 'you can go without any fear to receive your only true Friend'. Indeed, she sees that Jesus is offended not by Marie's supposed sin, but by her 'lack of confidence'. Thérèse then reiterates her favourite theme of love:

Your heart is made to love Jesus, to love him passionately; pray that the *beautiful years of your life* may not pass in chimerical fears. We have only the short moments of our life to love Jesus.

Finally, Thérèse deals with what was apparently another source of scruples for Marie: how to have a proper devotion to the Mother of God:

Have no fear of loving the Blessed Virgin *too much,* you will *never* love her enough, and Jesus will be pleased since the Blessed Virgin is his Mother.

This letter of the sixteen-year-old Thérèse shows exceptional maturity, despite its simple style. It also gives the heart of Thérèse's Eucharistic spirituality: love received and love returned.

It would be wrong to think of Thérèse's deep Eucharistic faith as something easily acquired. There is a very interesting text in her autobiography, which at first sight seems a trifle jejune. She recalled that in the early years of her religious life, 'contrary to my usual state of mind', she had a sense that God was not pleased with her. Since the Communion hosts at the time had been in somewhat short supply, she had been given recently only a half host. Then she thought:

I said to myself: Ah! if I receive only half a host today, this will cause me great sorrow, and I shall believe that Jesus comes regretfully into my heart. I approached, and oh, what joy! For the first time in my life I saw the priest take two hosts which were well separated and place them on my tongue! You can understand my joy and the sweet tears of consolation I shed when beholding a mercy so great.[28]

Thérèse's faith was often attacked. Just as she had not been spared scrupulosity, she did not escape some struggle in believing that the Lord was pleased with her efforts. She remarked at the same time:

You see, dear Mother, that I am far from being on the way of fear; I always find a way of being happy and of profiting from my miseries; no doubt this does not displease Jesus since He seems to encourage me on this road.[29]

Littleness and frailty are the foundations on which she built her spirituality.

Thanksgiving after Communion

Probably Thérèse's greatest contribution to spirituality was her discovery of what she called her 'Little Way'. It was a profound grasp of spiritual childhood, so that holiness of loving God was not a matter of great achievements, like those of the saints, but rather of doing small things well.[30] This Little Way is strikingly illustrated in another text that hides more than it reveals. She is speaking about thanksgiving after Communion. Mass and thanksgiving together occupied about an hour. Since we know how eager Thérèse was to receive Communion, what she says about thanksgiving may seem surprising. Unlike the Great Teresa of Avila, she notes that she did not receive special graces at the time after Communion:

I can't say that I frequently received consolations when making my thanksgivings after Mass; perhaps it is the time when I receive the least. However, I find this very understandable since I have offered myself to Jesus not as one desirous of her own consolation in His visit but simply to please Him who is giving himself to me.[31]

Thérèse shows herself here as having achieved a profound detachment. St Teresa of Avila never tired of warning her sisters that they are not to expect consolations, and especially not to be dependent or greedy in their regard. Thérèse is writing about a time about four years before her death when she had achieved a radical de-centering from herself to God. She is the one who serves totally out of love and not for any reward.

She then goes on to describe her preparation for Communion, before taking up again the question of thanksgiving:

> When I am preparing for Holy Communion, I picture my soul as a [*free, libre*] piece of land and I beg the Blessed Virgin to remove from it *any rubbish* that would prevent it from being *free;* then I ask her to set up a huge tent worthy of *heaven,* adorning it with *her own* jewellery; finally I invite all the angels and saints to come and conduct a magnificent concert there. It seems to me that when Jesus descends into my heart He is content to find Himself so well received and I, too, am content. All this, however, does not prevent both distractions and sleepiness from visiting me, but at the end of the thanksgiving when I see that I've made it so badly I make a resolution to be thankful throughout the rest of the day.[32]

There are several points to be made about this passage. Firstly, we see the total unselfishness in Thérèse's love: Communion for her is a way of loving Jesus, rather than receiving anything for herself. Secondly, the sense is a trifle distorted in the English translation, which omits the word 'free' about the piece of land, despite the fact that Thérèse had underlined it. There are surely Carmelite echoes in her imagery here. She wishes to have herself unencumbered – something of the 'nothing' (*nada*) of St John of the Cross – so as to be fully at the disposal of Jesus. Thirdly, we have the image of the tent that Mary is to set up for the reception of her Son. Thérèse had already used this image of the soul being like an empty tent prepared for the Lord's concert in a letter written in 1894 to Céline.[34] We have already seen the language of tabernacle, which is frequent in her Eucharistic reflections. Fourthly, we find here her profound sense of the Communion of Saints: those in heaven are united with our worship on earth, and we can always call upon their help, in this case Mary, the saints and angels. We see Thérèse not only invoking Mary's help, but in a profound sense being joined with her, so that the concerns of Mary and Thérèse are identified, making Jesus welcome. Thérèse here as in many other places shows the intimate relationship between her and the Mother of God.

However, the idea of invoking Mary in preparation for, or thanksgiving after Communion, is not novel. Each of the volumes of Guéranger's *Liturgical Year* has long acts of preparation and thanksgiving that invoke Mary and the saints at these moments.[35] In fact, one wonders if these are not among the prayers that Thérèse was thinking of in the passage we cited in chapter one about the 'beautiful prayers' that left her with a headache. Finally, we can take consolation from Thérèse's sleepiness during prayer, even if we may not always have as good an excuse. By the time of thanksgiving she had already been over two and a half hours at prayer[36] and this was in the days of strict Eucharistic fast.

The Communion preparation and thanksgiving of Thérèse might raise some questions for post-Vatican II liturgy. A welcome feature of the renewed liturgy is the opportunity for silent prayer after Communion. But the rubric is not very strong: 'After Communion, the priest and people may spend some time in silent prayer';[37] in parishes it is frequently either perfunctory or omitted. It would seem very difficult to appreciate the wonder of the Eucharist without some extended prayer. However, this may not always be possible and here Thérèse's practice is encouraging: she remains in thanksgiving for the rest of the day. Not very different is the thought of the German theologian, Karl Rahner, in an article he wrote a few years before Vatican II, 'On Developing Eucharistic Devotion'. Rahner is pastorally sensitive both to the difficulty of spending sufficient time in either preparation or thanksgiving, and to the danger of such insistence on appropriate time as might lead people to refrain from Mass or Communion. He suggests that thanksgiving is the preparation for the sacrifice in daily life of one who has shared in the sacrifice of Christ; it is in thanksgiving that there can be an 'encounter between the worship of God at the altar and the worship of God in life'.[38]

One might think that a cause of distress for Thérèse would have been the fact that she often slept during the time for thanksgiving after Communion. Her reaction is simple:

> Well, I am not desolate. I remember that *little children* are as pleasing to their parents when they are asleep as well as when they are awake; I remember, too that when they perform operations, doctors put their patients to sleep. Finally, I remember that: *'The Lord knows our weakness, that he is mindful that we are but dust and ashes.*[39]

Her Little Way once again enlightens her approach to prayer.

Intercession

Thérèse was utterly convinced of the power of the Eucharist for herself and others. There are some touching references to this conviction that are indications of Thérèse's fidelity to others. She recounted that when she was six she met an invalid to whom she sought to give alms. He refused her money with a smile; it was not what the man needed most. Thérèse said about the incident:

> I remembered having heard that on our First Communion day we can obtain whatever we ask for, and this thought greatly consoled me. Although I was only six years old at this time, I said: 'I'll pray for this poor man on the day of my First Communion.' I kept my promise five years later, and I hope that God answered the prayer he inspired me to direct to Him in favour of one of his suffering members.[40]

She had a similar fidelity in her prayer for a priest who had lost his way and left the Church, Fr Hyacinth Loyson. She offered what was to have been her last Communion for his conversion, a matter that had preoccupied her for many years.[41] We should look too in her letters to the future missionaries who had been committed to her prayer and her direction by letter, Fr Adolph Roulland, and the Abbé Bellière, whom she called her two missionary brothers. In 1895-1896 Thérèse was given these two to support through her prayer and correspondence. The seventeen letters she wrote to them contain some of her most profound teaching. She frequently asks them to remember her at Mass and Communion, and tells them that she prays for them on the same occasions.

A cause of great distress for her was, of course, being able to receive Communion only very seldom because of her illness. On the eve of the feast of Our Lady of Mount Carmel (16 July), it was suggested that she might die on the feast after receiving Communion. Thérèse's reply was robust:

> Oh, that wouldn't resemble my little way. Would you want me to leave this little way, then, in order to die? Dying after receiving Holy Communion would be too beautiful for me; little souls couldn't imitate this.

She only wished that she would be well enough to communicate, 'Otherwise God is obliged to return to the tabernacle; understand? (voyez-vous cela!)'[42]

Just as the disarming simplicity of Thérèse's attitude to her problem of sleepiness shows us that she finds an answer in being simple and childlike, so too she avoids becoming complicated in her intercessory prayer. How is she to pray at Mass for all the people she was concerned about with all their complicated needs? She could so easily forget something important. In the final pages of her autobiography, the *Story of a Soul*, she reflects:

> For simple souls there must be no complicated ways; as I am of their number, one morning during my thanksgiving, Jesus gave me a simple means of accomplishing my mission. He made me understand these words of the Canticle of Canticles: *'DRAW ME, WE SHALL RUN after you in the odour of your ointments.'* O Jesus, it is not even necessary to say: *'When drawing me, draw the souls whom I love!'* This simple statement: 'Draw me' suffices; I understand, Lord, that when a soul allows herself to be captivated by *the odour of your ointments,* she cannot run alone, all the souls whom she loves follow in her

train; this is done without constraint, without effort, it is a
natural consequence of her attraction for You.[43]

Here her 'Little Way,' indicated by the oblique 'simple souls', shows
that for Thérèse her deep and universal love did not lead to anxiety,
confusion or elaborate systems of prayer. The understanding of her
vocation as being 'love in the heart of the Church'[44] simplified
everything: she followed Jesus and he took over all her cares.

When she first wrote this passage, she used the intimate French
form of the pronoun *(tu)* referring to Jesus seven times in thirteen
lines; since she was writing for the rather stiffly formal Mother Marie
de Gonzague, she later changed these to the polite form of the
pronoun *(vous)*.[45] But her first instinct in recalling this insight was to
reflect the deep intimacy between her and the Lord.

We should not miss her clear awareness of having been given
special insight from God. Here she uses the phrase, 'he made me
understand' *(il m'a fait comprendre);* elsewhere she often employs a
French past definite verb, 'I understood' *(je compris),* in speaking of
special divine illumination. In our attempt to see the Little Way as
imitable, we need to be alert to the great graces and insights she
received. Such divine teaching was the reason why she would, in the
following century, be named the thirty-third doctor of the Church.[46]

The Mass

Since it is so central in the day of the Carmelite, there are rather few
references to Mass in her writings. In her letters to her missionary
brothers, the seminarian and priest who had been entrusted to her
care, she is deeply aware of their union through the Mass. Writing to
Fr Adolph Roulland, she writes with feigned innocence:

> If I did not fear to be indiscreet, I would ask you, Reverend
> Father, to make each day at the holy altar a memento for me.[47]

Later she would say how much joy it gave her to have a missionary
brother to remember her daily at the altar.[48]

Thérèse's understanding of the Mass emerges in a poem, 'My
Desires near Jesus Hidden in His Prison of Love.' It reflects a
nineteenth-century theology, with a strong emphasis on sacrifice.

She says,

> The Altar is a new Calvary
> Where His blood still flows for me.

But she develops her Eucharistic faith especially in a deep sense of the presence of Jesus and of her own union with him particularly in his sacrifice:

> Jesus, holy and sacred Vine,
> O my Divine King, You know
> I am a cluster of golden grapes
> Which must disappear for you.
> Under the wine press of suffering,
> I shall prove my love for you.
> I want no other joy
> Than to sacrifice myself each day.
> Ah! what joy, I am chosen
> Among the grains of pure Wheat
> Who lose their lives for Jesus.[49]

Her translator, Donald Kinney, notes that more than a dozen of her poems take up Eucharistic themes.[50] The dominant themes are those of the Eucharist being the sacrament of love, the love of Thérèse for her Eucharistic Lord, his delight in dwelling in human hearts.

The Eucharistic teaching of Thérèse, which we have seen in this chapter, is admirably summarised in the proper of the Mass for her feast on 30 September.[51] The opening prayer places before us the theme of littleness and invites us to follow her way:

> God our Father, you have promised your kingdom to those who are willing to become like little children. Help us to follow the way of St Thérèse with confidence so that by her prayers we may come to know your eternal glory.[52]

The Preface of this Mass sums up her life and message, and gives reasons why we today should give thanks to God:

Father, all powerful and everliving God . . . You reveal the secrets of your kingdom to those who become like little children. Among them you chose Saint Thérèse, hidden in Christ, to proclaim the good news of your merciful love. Your Holy Spirit moved her to make her life an oblation of prayer and self-denial for the salvation of all mankind through Christ and his Church. Now with the saints . . . [53]

This lyrical text seems at first sight to have four themes: the implicit citation of Matthew 11:25; Thérèse, the prophet of merciful love; her missionary spirit; the apostolic value of prayer and sacrifice. But it is really a canticle celebrating the contemplative life as a participation of the mission of Christ and the Church.[54] As such it encapsulates the Eucharistic teaching of Thérèse, which is found even more briefly in the Prayer after Communion:

Lord by the power of your love St Thérèse offered herself to you and prayed for the salvation of all.

6

Mental Prayer and Praying with Scripture

As we come to look further at the teaching of St Thérèse on prayer we run into some problems. The various forms of prayer have very different names, and it is easy to confuse them or to misunderstand them in a particular author. Here the difficulty is with a way of praying that in French Thérèse calls *oraison*, which we shall call 'mental prayer.' Since all prayer is surely mental, using our minds in some way, an immediate uncertainty can arise.

We all know what we mean by vocal prayers: these are prayers that we say. They are usually prayers that we have learned by heart, or perhaps found in a book or leaflet. They may also be the prayers of the liturgy or prayers that we make up ourselves. The next chapter will deal with the vocal prayer of Thérèse, whereas this one will be concerned with her other ways of praying and with her use of the scriptures in prayer.

Meditation and contemplative prayer

In the first part of the twentieth century and even before, meditation was used about a prayer method that originated with St Ignatius Loyola. But some distortions of Ignatian prayer arose that seemed to put more stress on the mechanics of praying than on love, which is its true meaning and ground. People emphasised the way in which imagination, intellect and will were to be applied to a topic in a methodical way. Often such exercises left little scope for the colloquy – speaking from one's heart with God, Mary or the saints – based on what one had reflected on. This colloquy, a sacred dialogue, is at the heart of Ignatian prayer. As a result of poor instruction in the rich prayer of Ignatius, many people were turned off the idea of meditation and especially the word. Today we find people talking about 'quiet prayer', 'reflective prayer' or some other term.

In its treatment of meditation, the *Catechism of the Catholic Church* stresses the activity of thought, imagination, emotion and desire.[1] It indicates that one should not stop at these but move on 'to the knowledge of the love of the Lord Jesus, to union with him.'[2] It further states:

> Meditation is a prayerful quest engaging thought, imagination, emotion and desire. Its goal is to make our own in faith the subject considered, by confronting it with the reality of our own life.[3]

This description of meditation leaves it rather much at the intellectual level. But the *Catechism* has another expression for prayer, which in its original French was called *oraison*, 'contemplative prayer'. It then asks: 'What is contemplative prayer?' and replies:

> St Teresa answers 'Contemplative prayer *[oración mental]* in my opinion is nothing else than a close sharing between friends; it means taking time frequently to be alone with him who we know loves us.' Contemplative prayer seeks him 'whom my soul loves' (Song of Songs 1:7; cf. 3:1–4). It is Jesus, and in him, the Father . . . In this inner prayer we can still meditate, but our attention is fixed on the Lord himself.[4]

Though its thought in the English translation is not fully clear, the *Catechism* would seem to imply that meditation is concerned with ourselves, with our grasp of the mysteries, whereas what it calls 'contemplative prayer' is rather more a reaching towards the person of Jesus and the Trinity.

In the case of Thérèse we need to stand back a trifle from the language of the *Catechism*, and concentrate more on how she prayed than on what words she used to describe what ensued when she was alone with God. We will see that she prayed in ways that the *Catechism* calls 'meditation' and 'contemplative prayer' – though we shall continue to use the words 'mental prayer' for the latter. The distinction is not always clear-cut in her writings, but by examining what she says we can learn about her rich prayer. So we look successively at three ideas in Thérèse: meditation, mental prayer, and the scripture, this last at times straddling both kinds of prayer.

Thérèse and Meditation
In an earlier chapter we saw that even as a child Thérèse was attracted to some prayer that was deeper than vocal prayer. It is not easy to determine exactly what she means in every statement; like many other authors her mature grasp of prayer clearly influences the way in which she interprets her childhood efforts. Still, the attempt to see how she uses language will help us to appreciate the simple yet profound nature of her prayer, even in childhood.

Thérèse does not use the word 'meditate' *(méditer)* very frequently. Occasionally it has the common meaning of 'think at length about'. But there are more significant usages. She speaks of a time when she went fishing with her father. Sometimes she fished, but she says,

> I preferred to go *alone* and sit down on the grass bedecked with flowers, and then my thoughts became very profound indeed! Without knowing what it was to meditate, my soul was absorbed in real prayer. I listened to distant sounds, the murmuring of the wind, etc. At times, the indistinct notes of some military music reached me where I was, filling my heart with a sweet melancholy. Earth then seemed to be a place of exile and I could dream only of heaven.[5]

We do not know exactly when this happened, but it was probably before Thérèse was eight. There are some tantalising details in the little passage. One wonders at the phrase 'very profound thoughts indeed'. We know that Thérèse indulged in a gentle self-mockery throughout her life. It is hard to know whether or not she is being whimsical here. She is clear that what she was engaged in was real prayer, and she implies that it was meditation. The kind of prayer here seems not unlike what the *Catechism* calls 'meditation,' when it speaks of praying with 'the book of life'.[6] We should note too her use of the word 'heaven' *(ciel):* Thérèse was fascinated both by the sky and by heaven. The word *ciel* occurs over seven hundred times in her writings, as well as over sixty times in her sayings taken down by Mother Agnes and others and published as *Last Conversation.*

She tells us that she meditated on the leaflet 'On Renunciation' that her sister Marie had given her in preparation for First Communion.[7] She liked at that time to be alone in her room for hours on end to study and to meditate.[8]

There is an interesting passage about prayer when she recalls her impatience to make her first profession in the convent:

> I was to wait for another eight months. I found it difficult, at first, to accept this great sacrifice, but soon light shone in my soul. I was meditating on *(je méditais)* the foundations of the spiritual life by Father Surin at the time. One day, during my prayer *(oraison)*, I understood *(je compris)* that my intense desire to make Profession was mixed with a great self-love. Since I had given myself to Jesus to please and console him, I had no right to oblige Him to do my will instead of His own. I understood, too *(je compris encore)*, that a fiancée should be adorned for her wedding day, and I myself was doing absolutely nothing about this. Then I said to Jesus: 'O my God! I don't ask you to make profession. I will wait as long as you desire, but what I don't want is to be the cause of my separation from you through my fault . . .'[9]

There are quite a few points that might be made about this apparently simple little incident. Firstly, we should note the difficulty, disappointment and struggle associated with the postponement of her profession. It is a natural reaction, and Thérèse is not ashamed of it. She is already beginning to regard the setback in religious terms – she calls it 'a great sacrifice'. Secondly, she tells us that at the time she was meditating on a book by Fr J. J. Surin called *The Foundations of the Spiritual Life drawn from The Imitation of Christ*, which had been published 150 years earlier in Paris. She probably means by 'meditating' that she was studying it carefully and reflecting on it – otherwise she would probably have used the ordinary word, 'I was reading'. Spiritual reading, that is, reflective reading of a spiritual book, was a normal feature of Carmelite life. It is notable also that Surin's was a book based on her especially favourite work, *The Imitation of Christ*. It was from this book that she first read about detachment; she called its contents 'pure wheat'.[10] Later she would draw the same doctrine, even more profoundly, from St John of the Cross.[11] Thirdly, this act of meditating over a period *(je méditais)* left her open to enlightenment. She tells us that when at mental prayer *(oraison)*, she understood *(je compris,* used twice*)*. As we have already noted this expression is frequently used by Thérèse to indicate some light she received from God; indeed elsewhere she frequently uses the word 'light' or 'lights' for the same reality, as when a few lines lower she says, 'I had already received, since taking the habit, abundant lights *(d'abundantes lumières)* on religious profession.'[12] Fourthly, we should note that for Thérèse, prayer and life were integrated. She was reflecting, then she received light at prayer time, about her attitude to a disappointment. Finally, we can see her reaction to the light. The inspiration she received at prayer was twofold: her desire for immediate profession was tinged with selfishness; she had not been preparing appropriately. She immediately surrenders her will, breaking into spontaneous prayer from the heart.

Saint Thérèse seems to use the word 'meditate' for reflection, especially when it relates the divine mysteries to her own life. Thus about the text of John 15:13 on the greater love that is laying down one's life, she remarks:

> [W]hen meditating upon these words of Jesus, I understood *(j'ai compris)* how imperfect was my love for my Sisters. I saw that I didn't love them as God loves them . . .[13]

Though it is sometimes interchangeable with meditation, the term 'mental prayer' *(oraison)* has a very profound content for Thérèse. As we move to consider it, it is sometimes important to remember that the word that we translate as 'mental prayer' *(oraison)* was also used in the horarium, or daily timetable, for the hour set aside in the morning and evening for personal prayer.

Thérèse and mental prayer

Writing to her missionary brother, Fr Roulland, Thérèse brings together three important ideas that allow us insight into how she prayed: mental prayer, meditation and the bible:

> This evening, during my prayer *(oraison)* I meditated on some passages from Isaiah which appeared to me so appropriate for you that I cannot refrain from copying them for you.

She then writes out Is 54:2–3 and 60:4–5.[14] She would have obtained these texts from the notebook that Céline had brought with her to the Carmel in 1884. She describes her activity at the time of mental prayer *(oraison)* as meditating on Isaiah. Not only that but she made the connection with Fr Roulland's impending departure to China. Meditation is again related to life.

We can see further connections in an important passage probably from 1895, when she had already discovered her Little Way. Moreover, it gives us some indications of the sources of Thérèse's prayer.

> Ah! how many lights have I not drawn from the works of our holy Father, St John of the Cross! At the ages of seventeen and eighteen I had no other spiritual nourishment; later on, however, all books left me in aridity and I'm still in that state. If I open a book composed by a spiritual author (even the most beautiful, the most touching book), I feel my heart contract immediately and I read without understanding, so to speak. Or if I do understand, my mind comes to a standstill without the capacity of meditating *(sans pouvoir méditer)*. In this helplessness, Holy Scripture and the *Imitation* come to my aid; in them I discover solid and very *pure* nourishment. But it is especially the gospel that sustains me during my hours of prayer *(pendant mes oraisons)*, for in them I find what is

necessary for my poor little soul. I am constantly discovering in them new lights, hidden and mysterious meanings.

She goes on to speak of lights,

> Never have I heard Him [Jesus] speak, but I feel that He is within me, at each moment, He is guiding and inspiring me with what I must say and do. I find just when I need them certain lights that I had not seen until then, and it isn't most frequently during my hours of prayer *(pendant mes oraisons)* that these are most abundant but rather in the midst of my daily occupations.[15]

We can learn a lot from this passage. She says that for two years her main guide was St John of the Cross. We know that she imbibed not only the hard doctrine of the *Ascent of Mount Carmel* and the *Dark Night,* but also the mystical doctrine of the *Spiritual Canticle* and *The Living Flame.* It seems that now, probably in 1895, two years before her death, St John of the Cross is no longer so enlightening, though she continues to quote him, especially from the last two works, in parts of the autobiography written about this time and in her letters and poems.

In her present state of aridity, which would in fact largely last until her death, she obtains light only from the Gospels and *The Imitation of Christ.* She speaks of them as 'solid and very pure nourishment'. Earlier she contrasted the pure wheat of the *Imitation* with another book that helped her a great deal, but which she called 'honey and oil in abundance', the conferences of the Abbé Arminjon that we have mentioned in chapter two.[16]

She tells us also that spiritual books were not of any help 'to meditate', but the Gospels and the *Imitation* apparently were. She uses the Gospel for the time of mental prayer *(oraison).* She discovers 'new lights, hidden and mysterious meanings'. As is clear in the same passage, these illuminations are graced: they are teachings she received from Jesus. Thérèse then expands her thought about such divine insights. She has them when it is needed, but significantly rarely at the times of prayer. They come in the midst of her daily work. In Catholic spiritual theology, especially as exemplified by St Ignatius Loyola, there is a special value to be attached to graces that come unexpectedly. Ignatius calls them 'consolations without any previous cause'.[17] Since we have made no contribution to receiving such graces, there is a higher certainty that they are from God. Thus if I am praying, I am disposed to have spiritual thoughts; more significant are illuminations that come when I am sweeping a floor, folding an umbrella or trimming toenails.

It seems clear at this stage that she does not distinguish carefully the meaning of the words that she uses about her prayer. She is more concerned with meeting the Lord's will than with the precise method. Continuing in this vein, it will be helpful to look at her use of the scriptures to learn more about her prayer.

Thérèse and scripture

We know that Thérèse had a great love of the scriptures.[18] In declaring her a doctor of the Church, Pope John Paul II stressed that 'the primary source of her spiritual experience and her teaching is the Word of God in the Old and New Testaments.'[19] We have a valuable testimony of her sister Céline (Sr Geneviève) at the investigation prior to beatification of Thérèse:

> [Thérèse] nourished her soul on the Sacred Scriptures. From childhood she also liked the *Imitation* very much, and knew it by heart. But what she used most of all in prayer was the Holy Gospel. She even carried this sacred book around next to her heart, and used to go to considerable trouble to find editions of the individual gospels, which she then bound together so that others could do as she did. She studied the Bible in order 'to find out what God was like' *(connaître le caractère du bon Dieu)*. The differences between the various translations bothered her: 'If I had been a priest,' she used to say, 'I would have studied Hebrew and Greek really well in order to know the divine thinking exactly as God deigned to express it in human language.'[20]

The differences of translations really seem to have caused her quite a lot of anxiety. In this passage, her sisters says that it bothered her *(l'affligeait)*. In the *Last Conversations,* her sister Agnes quotes her as saying that it was sad to see the differences of translation.[21]

In our post-Vatican II era, it can still be a surprise to learn that nuns in Thérèse's time did not have access to the whole bible. The Old Testament was regarded as inappropriate at least for younger sisters. We do not know what, if any, access Thérèse may have had to the family bible whilst at home. Before Céline entered Carmel and while still looking after her father, she copied into a notebook long extracts from the Old Testament. She gave this to Thérèse and we know that it was in this hand-written book that Thérèse discovered the texts that led her to her Little Way.[22] Céline testifies that these pages proved to be 'delicious nourishment for her mental prayer'.[23] Thérèse also studied whatever passages came her way in the Missal, translations of the Divine Office and other books that contained scriptural citations, such as Guéranger's *Liturgical Year.*[24] As a result, her texts are sometimes somewhat freely translated; her accuracy was only as good as her sources.

Various people have testified to Thérèse's love of the scriptures and the deep insights she drew from them. Her novice mistress stated that 'she had an unusually keen understanding of the Sacred Scriptures – a thing readily apparent from the way she uses them in her writings.'[25] Another sister stated at the beatification process that she cited scripture constantly 'and with such aptness that one would have said that her conversation was only a commentary on the sacred books'.[26] Again Céline recalled:

> At Carmel the Bible was her greatest treasure, and it was with amazing ease and keen perception that she was able to assimilate various passages of Holy Writ; she found no difficulty in discovering their hidden meaning and then in applying the lesson in an unusual way.[27]

Céline also said at the beatification process that what 'occupied her above all during mental prayer was meditation on the Holy Gospel.'[28] Another beatification witness, Sr Thérèse de Saint-Augustin stated:

> She took delight in the Holy Scripture. She was never at a loss in choosing passages which best suited people. It was clear that she nourished herself each day on the scripture.[29]

Though Thérèse studied the scriptures carefully, we do not have the sense that she looked at commentaries, even those that were available to her. Perhaps she did. But what is much clearer is a special gift she received of being able to penetrate the meaning of God's Word, so that it became alive for her. This gift is quite widespread among all Christians who approach the Bible with an open mind and a pure heart.

It can be asked: how did she use the scriptures in her prayer time? Here we can usefully look at the Carmelite tradition, before garnering some indications from Thérèse herself. The Carmelite *Rule* does not give much indication about how the scriptures were to be used, save that reflection on them was to be a constant occupation of the Carmelite:

> Each of you is to stay in his own cell or nearby, pondering the Lord's law day and night and keeping watch at his prayers unless attending to some other duty.[30]

The compressed verses of Ps 119 [118]:100, 105, 60 that she quotes towards the end of her life show the depth of her appropriation of the spirit of the Carmelite *Rule:*

> In the same Psalm 118, [David] does not hesitate to add: *'I have had understanding above old men, because I have sought your will. Your word is a lamp for my feet. I am prepared to carry out your commandments and I am TROUBLED ABOUT NOTHING.'* [31]

Thérèse is very conscious of being enlightened by the Word of God. We can see this in several ways. Firstly, verses of the scripture strike her profoundly. Thus even when she was fourteen she tells us:

> The cry of Jesus on the Cross sounded continually in my heart:
> *'I thirst!'* These words ignited within me an unknown and very
> living fire. I wanted to give my Beloved to drink and I felt
> myself consumed with a *thirst for souls.*[32]

A parallel may be detected when she recalls her pilgrimage to Rome
at the age of fourteen. She had got nowhere with her request to
diocesan authorities to enter Carmel at fifteen. Now at the papal
audience, where protocol demanded that she should not speak to the
Pope, she dared to ask him about her entry to Carmel. She said that,
at the papal Mass,

> My heart beat strongly and my prayers were fervent when Jesus
> descended into the hands of His Pontiff. However, I was filled
> with confidence, for the Gospel of that day contained these
> beautiful words, 'Fear not, little flock, for it is your Father's
> good pleasure to give you the kingdom' (Luke 12:32).[33]

The significance of such texts – and there are plenty of similar ones
– is obvious in the light of the teaching of St Teresa of Avila. In the
Interior Castle she is discussing the discernment of inner words, in
particular how one can be sure that they are from God. She offers
three signs: the word is effective, doing what it says; it brings a
profound peace and it is never forgotten.[34]

It would not seem that Thérèse received the kind of special
communication that Teresa calls locutions. But the enlightenment
that she so frequently received from the scripture would seem to be a
chief way in which God communicated to her. And in her case we do
find that the signs of which Teresa of Avila speaks were present.[35] In
the first text she is filled with thirst; in the second she has confidence
to speak to the Pope. Again, the Word of God speaks deeply within
her, so that she is left with profound peace. And finally, these special
enlightenments of scripture are burned into her memory, so that even
when she recalls them years later, they seem as fresh as when she
received the special light.

A second feature of her use of the scriptures was her habit of
seeking answers in them. She tells us explicitly that when faced with

two great problems she searched the scriptures for an answer. One question revolved around how to be holy, since the ways of the great saints appeared to be beyond her. She searched and found the two texts (Prov 9:4 and Isaiah 66:13, 12) that would lead her to her Little Way.[36]

Another major question that deeply affected her arose from her unlimited desires to serve God. At her prayer-time she said,

> my desires caused me a veritable martyrdom, and I opened the Epistles of St Paul to find some kind of answer. Chapters 12 and 13 fell under my eyes and I read there in the first of these chapters that all cannot be apostles, prophets, doctors etc. . . . The answer was clear, but it did not fulfil my desires and gave me no peace. . . . Without becoming discouraged, I continued my reading, and this sentence consoled me, 'Yet strive after the better gifts . . .'

After reading this she says, 'I finally had rest.' She immediately goes on to share all the lights she received, using the phrase 'I understood' *(je compris)* three times before crying out joyfully her discovery, 'My vocation is love.'[37] Here again God spoke to her through the scriptures, and again the signs given by Teresa of Avila are all present.

This enlightenment in her prayer through the Word of God raises another question. It is clear that she searched the scriptures for answers to her problems. The last text we have cited even gives the impression that she was used to such searching and to receiving an answer. Another example is found in a letter to Céline, shortly before the latter's entry to Carmel:

> After reading your letter, I went to prayer *(à l'oraison)*, and taking the gospel, I asked Jesus to find a passage for you, and this is what I found: 'Behold the fig tree and the other trees, when they begin to bear leaves [...] know that the kingdom of God is near.' I closed the book, I had read enough; in fact, *these things* taking place in my Céline's soul prove the kingdom is set up in her soul.[38]

Thérèse then goes on to share what was happening in her at the time. It brings us a bit away from our immediate concern, which is Thérèse and the scriptures, but it gives such a rich teaching on prayer that we might gather its riches in passing. She felt that since Jesus did not seem to be asking anything specific from her,

> I had to go along quietly in peace and love, doing only what he was asking me. . . . But I had a light. St Teresa says we must maintain love. The *wood* is not within our reach when we are in darkness, in aridities, but are we not obliged to throw little pieces of straw on it?

Thérèse refers here to a common experience in the spiritual life, when nothing much seems to be happening; moreover she is in darkness. Whilst as it were remaining quietly and contentedly in this state, she had a light. She does not say that she thought about it and made a discovery: lights for Thérèse were usually a special insight that she regards as a lift. The insight is that she must continue to be active, despite the aridity and darkness. The fire can be fed with little pieces of straw. She says that such actions please Jesus, who then stokes the fire himself and we feel the heat of love. Then she continues,

> I have experienced it; when I *am feeling* nothing, when I am INCAPABLE *of praying*, of practising virtue, then this is the moment for seeking opportunities, *nothings*, which please Jesus more than mastery of the world or even martyrdom suffered with generosity. For example, a smile, a friendly word, when I want to say nothing, or put on a look of annoyance, etc., etc. [. . .]When I do not have opportunities, I want to tell Him frequently that I love Him; this is not difficult, and it keeps the *fire* going. *Even though* this fire of love would seem to me to have gone out, I would like to throw something on it, and Jesus could then relight it [. . .] I am not always faithful, but I never get discouraged; I abandon myself into the arms of Jesus.[39]

This letter was written in July 1893. It would still be more than a year before she articulated her Little Way, but its elements are already present – telling Jesus of her love, little almost insignificant acts of love for others, confidence and abandonment in her weakness. In this text we see again her ability to relate what she read in the Bible to her life situation.

We know that in the Carmels at the time there was a practice of opening the scriptures at random to seek light and guidance. As Thérèse began writing in obedience the *Story of a Soul*, she invoked the help of Mary to guide her.

> I begged her to guide my hand that it trace no line displeasing to her. Then opening the Holy Gospels my eyes fell on these words, 'And going up a mountain he called to him men of his *own choosing* and they came to him' (Mk 3:13). This is the mystery of my vocation, my whole life, and especially the mystery of the privileges Jesus showered on my soul.[40]

This short text is seen to have special depth and riches for her – summing up her whole life. Here there is clearly more than biblical scholarship, such as one might find in a commentary. It is not the meaning of the sacred author, the literal sense; yet it has a profound meaning for Thérèse. The Spirit speaks to her in and through the text, so that the inspired Word becomes a word to her inner being.

But this practice of opening the scriptures is not without some dangers. In the contemporary Charismatic Renewal and in Pentecostal circles generally, people frequently open the scriptures. At times the aptness of the text can be quite dramatic; what in some groups is called 'an anointed opening' can be a very powerful intervention of the Holy Spirit. But there are also times when people open and find nothing, or would seem to misapply what they find. Again, there is need for discernment. The ultimate criterion can only be the Lord's: 'By their fruits . . .' (Mt 7:17–20). If a person opens and the Spirit is neither directing the search, nor helping with the interpretation of the passage, it may not do either much harm or much good. Such texts are quickly forgotten. One cannot at all times demand or even expect divine guidance when randomly opening the scriptures. But there are times when God seems to work in this way.

The fruit in each case will most likely be in conformity with the three signs of St Teresa of Avila: it will be a word of power effecting what it says and it will bring peace and be deeply implanted in the memory.

The Carmelites also opened the scriptures at random to seek a passage for meditation or mental prayer. We may presume that Thérèse frequently did so too. However she encountered the Word of God, she applied it to life situations and it often gave her new lights, and that led to deepened love.

Another feature of Thérèse's use of the scriptures was her habit of repeating over and over some phrase that gave her guidance, light or comfort. Thus she says about her second Communion:

> My tears flowed again with an ineffable sweetness, and I repeated to myself these words of St Paul: 'It is no longer I that live, it is Jesus who lives in me!'[41]

Many schools of spirituality recommend the repetition of the scriptures, especially to savour the text and allow it to be deeply imprinted in the mind and heart. Some authors even speak of ruminating the text, going over and over it in one's mind and heart, like a contented animal chewing the cud. Thérèse knows another form of repetition, though the example is not from the scriptures but her beloved *Imitation*:

> Often during my Communions, I repeated these words of the *Imitation*: 'O Jesus, unspeakable *sweetness*, change all the consolations of this earth into bitterness for me.' This prayer fell from my lips without effort, without constraint; it seemed I repeated it not with my will but like a child who repeats the words a person he loves has inspired in him.[42]

This text refers to a period when Thérèse was about ten years old. It shows a remarkable prayer gift, known in the mystical tradition, where the word is implanted in a person without their effort.

Another feature of Thérèse's love relationship with the scriptures is that she continually finds new depth in them. In the last months of her life she had significant fresh insights into the Canticle of Canticles, so that she said she would like to write a commentary on it. She only managed a few pages, which makes us only too conscious of what we are missing. Significantly too, she indicates the sources of her insights, as she begins, 'He made me understand these words of the Canticle of Canticles: "Draw me, we shall run after the odour of your ointments"' (Cant 1:3).[43] She is quite conscious of her indebtedness to Jesus, mentioned in the previous sentence: 'it was He who made me understand' *(il m'a fait comprendre).*

Still more remarkable is her developed understanding of the command to love, which figures so prominently in the last part of her autobiography. She begins:

> This year, dear Mother, God has given me the grace to understand what charity is; I understood it before, it is true, but in an imperfect way. I never fathomed the meaning of these words of Jesus: *'The second commandment is LIKE the first: You shall love your neighbour as yourself.'* I applied myself to *loving God*, and it was in loving Him that I understood my love was not to be expressed only in words.[44]

She goes on to cite the new commandment 'love one another as I have loved you' (Jn 13:34) before developing a magnificent short treatise on the love of Jesus for his disciples, on how imperfect she discovered her love within community was, and the utterly simple ways in which supreme charity can be expressed.[45] Towards the end of this section she again shows that these insights are not her own, as she remarks, 'I am going to finish explaining what Jesus makes me understand *(m'a fait comprendre)* concerning charity.'[46] So what we have here is an initial insight – Jesus made her understand – followed by reflection on her concrete situation leading to conclusions that she ascribes to the Lord's guidance. She is in dialogue with the scriptures, with Jesus, and with her own reality.

The scriptures were not always alight with meaning for her. Thérèse also knew what it was to find the scriptures dry and arid. Writing to Céline she tells her about a passage, 'which expresses perfectly what a soul is when plunged into aridity and how nothing delights or consoles it'. She goes on:

> Frequently, we descend into fertile valleys where our heart loves to nourish itself, *the vast field of the scriptures* which has so many times opened before us to pour out its rich treasures in our favour; this *vast field* seems to us to be a desert, arid and without water. . . . We *know no longer* where *we are;* instead of peace and light, we find only turmoil or at least darkness.[47]

This long letter from 1894 goes on to give a profound theology of spiritual trials. It contains over twenty scriptural allusions or citations. Her writing so often seems to justify a happy phrase used about St John of the Cross, applied to her by Mgr Guy Gaucher, the Discalced Carmelite, presently bishop at Lisieux: 'He does not cite scripture, he incorporates it.'[48]

Conclusion

How much the wiser are we then about the prayer of Thérèse? We have seen that it was very rich, that it had times of great insight, times of aridity. The Bible had a central place in her prayer and she certainly had a special charism in its regard: the scriptures opened for her as they had to the two disciples on the Emmaus journey who exclaimed: 'Were not our hearts burning within us while he was talking to us on the road, while he was opening the scriptures to us?' (Lk 24:32; see v. 45).

Thérèse was not concerned with methods of mental prayer. Prayer for her was not an exercise but an expression of love. She would not care if she was engaged in meditation or mental prayer: she prayed only to please her beloved. From her we can learn that prayer is ultimately simple even though its expressions are varied. Above all we see that our focus should be not on our act of praying, but on the Lord who is drawing us to love him and one another.

7

Prayers of Thérèse

St Thérèse is a teacher of prayer in several senses. We have already seen something of what she wrote about liturgical prayer, about the Eucharist and about mental prayer. We can learn too from what she said about vocal prayer. There are a number of prayers that she wrote or dictated on various occasions for herself and others. It has been said that these twenty-one prayers, some very brief, 'contain the full message of Thérèse in miniature'.[1] In this chapter we shall see what she has said about vocal prayer before considering some of the formal prayers that she has written.

Saying prayers
The first thing we learn about prayer as children is about 'saying our prayers'. It is something that should be done; to omit 'saying my prayers' was a common sin, even a convenient one when searching for something to confess: 'I did not say my morning and evening prayer.' Prayer at regular times is a feature of all the great religions; the Jews pray several times a day, the Moslems have five prayer times. Many religions have set prayers that are to be said.

Catholics have been accustomed to think of four main ways of praying. The highest form of prayer is adoration, which worships God as Supreme Being and Creator. Thanksgiving is directed to God in return for good things that we have received. The proper response of sinful people is satisfaction through which we acknowledge our guilt and express our sorrow for having turned from God. Lastly, there is the prayer of petition by which we ask from God for what ourselves and others need. The great source for these main forms of prayer, as well as for others, is the book of Psalms, which expresses the whole human condition.

There are examples of all kinds of prayer in Thérèse's writings. But more significant than the specific examples of her prayer is her disposition, her attitude to God in prayer. It is perhaps particularly in her prayer that she teaches us her Little Way and the easy relationship we should have with God who loves us as his children. St Thérèse's doctrine of spiritual childhood is a most profound basis for all prayer. Moreover, it simplifies prayer and avoids much of the anxiety that can surround it.

Learning to pray

Prayer is not something natural like breathing. It is more like walking or talking, which we have to learn. If we cease to walk for a period, for example in illness, our muscles atrophy and it is difficult to begin walking again. If we do not use a language that we have learned it becomes first rusty and then is forgotten. Similarly, we need to keep in practice with prayer; learning prayer is something that we begin in this life and will perfect only in eternity.

There are no experts on prayer; in its regard even the greatest saints are still pupils at school. One meets few people who are satisfied with the way they pray. Many people have a sense of guilt, a vague feeling that they do not do it right, and they would like to learn how to pray 'properly'. There is also a way of learning to pray from the example of others.

The great lesson on prayer is to be found in the gospel: Jesus has been praying. It must surely have been wonderful to look at the Lord in prayer. When he concludes his prayer, one of the disciples shows how impressed he was by his request, 'Lord, teach us to pray' and adds 'as John taught his disciples' (Lk 11:1). And the Lord immediately teaches the 'Our Father' (Lk 11:1–4).

Meaning our prayer

If prayer is conversation with God – a dialogue in which we need both to listen and to speak – then obviously it is important to mean what we say. There are many prayer forms and the issue of meaning them arises in each. There are privileged prayers, namely the prayers that are inspired by the Spirit and are contained in the Sacred Scriptures. These prayers are God's own teaching about how to pray.

They are, therefore, the supreme models of prayer. In addition to the psalms there are prayers found throughout the Old and New Testaments. There are prayers that have a special approbation by the Church. These are prayers that have been approved for liturgy and other occasions. There are also other prayers composed by people and often having some Church approval, for instance the *imprimatur* or permission to print from the local bishop. Finally there are prayers that we compose ourselves, often spontaneously.

If we are saying prayers written by someone else, even by the Holy Spirit, there can be a special difficulty about meaning what we pray. Thérèse felt this quite acutely, and we can begin to seek her help precisely with this area of concern.

Thérèse's 'Treatise on Prayer'

What makes Thérèse so much a favourite with people is the fact that she admits to sharing experiences that are common to us all. We can easily identify with her struggle to love those who were difficult; we have all at some time fallen asleep at prayer; we have suffered disappointments and frustrations in trying to be good; we know what it is to fail. We may be quick to identify with these experiences of Thérèse's. Her solution for problems associated with vocal prayer is unique, and very simple. It is found in what we could consider her 'treatise on prayer' – less than five hundred words on prayer written in the last days of June or early in July 1897, that is, three months before her death. Though she was already desperately ill, she was at the height of her spiritual maturity. It is not, of course, a treatise properly so-called, but one can continually return to these two pages of her manuscript to plumb their depths further. In earlier chapters we have already considered some sentences from the account which follows, but at this point, it will perhaps be helpful to see the passage in its entirety and to follow the logic of its thought.

Thérèse is writing for Mother Marie de Gonzague whom, she recalls, had advised a novice that the Carmelite vocation was much more about praying than about writing letters. Thérèse then launches into her reflection on prayer. Since it is a crucial text, we copy exactly punctuation marks and ellipsis points (...) and restore the order of various phrases to correspond to her original text.

How great is the power of *Prayer!* One could call it a queen
who has at each instant free access to the King and who is able
to obtain whatever she asks. To be heard it is not necessary to
read from a book some beautiful formula composed for the
occasion. If this were the case. . . . alas! I would have to be
pitied! . . . Outside the *Divine Office,* which I am very
unworthy to recite, I do not have the courage to force myself
to search out *beautiful* prayers in books. It gives me a
headache, there are so many of them it really gives me a
headache! . . . And then each prayer is more *beautiful* than the
others . . . I cannot recite them all and not knowing which to
choose, I do like children who do not know how to read, I say
very simply to God what I wish to say, without composing
beautiful sentences, and he always understands me. . . . For
me, *prayer* is an aspiration of the heart, it is a simple glance
directed to Heaven, it is a cry of gratitude and love in the midst
of trial as well as in the midst of joy; finally it is something
great, supernatural *(surnaturel)*, which expands my soul and
unites me to Jesus.

However, I would not want you to believe, dear Mother,
that I recite without devotion the prayers said in common in
the choir or the hermitages. On the contrary, I love very
much these prayers in common, for Jesus has promised *to be
in the midst of those who gather together in His name.* I feel
then that the fervour of my Sisters makes up for my lack of
fervour; but when I am alone (I am ashamed to admit it) the
recitation of the rosary is more difficult for me than the
wearing of an instrument of penance. . . . I feel that I have
said this so poorly! I force myself in vain to meditate on the
mysteries of the rosary; I don't succeed in fixing my mind on
them. . . . For a long time I was desolate about this lack of
devotion that astonished me, for I love the Blessed Virgin so
much *(j'aime tant la Sainte Vierge)* that it should be easy for
me to recite in her honour prayers that are so pleasing to her.
Now I am less desolate; I think that the Queen of heaven,
since she is *my MOTHER,* must see my good will and she is
satisfied with it.

> Sometimes when my mind is in such great aridity that it is impossible to draw from it *(d'en tirer)* one single thought to unite me with God, I very slowly recite an 'Our Father' and then the angelic salutation; then these prayers give me great delight; they nourish my soul much more than if I had recited them precipitately a hundred times . . . [2]

There are a few preliminary points that might help us to grasp this passage. As we have said, its immediate context is the fact that Thérèse recalls that a novice who felt the need to write letters to do good had just found her prayer answered. The instant answer to the novice's prayer is not unlike Thérèse's own experience when as a fourteen-year-old she prayed for the conversion of Pranzini, who had been sentenced to death for a triple murder and appeared quite unrepentant. She saw an immediate and dramatic answer to her prayer in his conversion on the scaffold. Recalling it later, Thérèse saw that God was awakening her zeal and showing her that her desire to pray for sinners was pleasing to him.[3] God often gives such an answer to prayer to develop our zeal and our faith – later we may have to 'ask, search and knock' with perseverance (see Luke 11:5–13), even when heaven seems unheeding.

Another preliminary point might be borne in mind. It is useful to keep in mind the thoughts on prayer of St Teresa of Avila, whom Thérèse echoes several times here. In monasteries of Discalced Carmelites the works of St Teresa were a primary source for novitiate formation. This was especially true of her *Life* and the *Way of Perfection,* which Thérèse cites directly seven and thirteen times respectively in her writings.

The passage we have called a treatise begins by Thérèse marvelling at the power of prayer and its effectiveness: like a queen it can obtain what it desires. The editor of the critical edition, Conrad De Meester, suggests that she may well be thinking here of Queen Esther, who was able to save her people through pleading with King Ahasuerus (Esth 5:3–5). Moreover, St John of the Cross refers to this same passage from the Old Testament saying that those who achieve union with God 'obtain what they desire'.[4] Though at this point Thérèse is recalling a prayer answered immediately and with unexpected results, we have to remember that she also knew what it was to have to wait for an answer even to have had prayers apparently unheard. She prayed for her father's recovery, but it was not to be. She prayed for her sister Léonie's vocation with the Visitation Sisters, sure that her prayer would be answered.[5] But Léonie would succeed in being a religious only after Thérèse's death in a fourth attempt in 1899. She constantly prayed for her cousin, Jeanne, to have a child. Thérèse's intercessory prayer very frequently reflected the prayer of Martha in the bible, 'Lord, he whom you love is ill' (Jn 11:3). Thus she wrote to Jeanne:

> I assure you, dear Jeanne, that if you are not forgetting the littlest of your sisters, she, too, thinks very often of you, and you know that for a Carmelite to remember and especially to love is to pray. My poor prayers undoubtedly are not worth much, however, I hope that Jesus will answer them, and instead of looking at her who is addressing them to Him, He will rest His eyes on those who are their object, and thus He will be obliged to grant me all my requests.[6]

But there was no immediate answer to these prayers.[7] Later she wrote a sensitive poem that comforted her cousin.[8] But it was only on reading the first edition of Thérèse's *Story of a Soul* that Jeanne eventually came into peace about remaining childless. At the Apostolic Process for Thérèse's beatification, Jeanne recalled that she often invoked Thérèse in trials but they seemed to increase, and then she asked for the grace to bear them in a Christian way.[9]

Returning to Thérèse's little treatise on prayer, we note that she was not very concerned with seeking out beautiful prayers for some occasion. In her time very flowery prayers were much in vogue. Even the prayers given by the scholarly Guéranger in his *Liturgical Year* were rather effusive. Thérèse feels that she cannot choose from among the available prayers. So she finds a simple way: 'I say very simply to God what I want to say, without composing beautiful sentences, and he always understands me.'[10] Here we can surely hear an echo of St Teresa of Avila, who memorably described mental prayer as 'nothing else than an intimate sharing between friends'.[11]

Thérèse immediately goes on to give her famous description of prayer, which we have already considered in earlier chapters. Here we might underline two characteristics of her prayer: she describes it as a cry of gratitude and love in the midst of both trial and joy. The other obvious note here is her typical self-forgetfulness. And so, gratitude and love are centred on God; she expresses both in her trials and joy. She continues: 'finally it is something great, supernatural, which expands my soul and unites me to Jesus.'[12] One can with confidence point to Teresa of Avila as a source for this thought. The word 'supernatural' has a specific meaning in the Spanish saint's works: it means what we would rather call 'mystical', that is, given by God as a special grace.[13] The effects that Thérèse observes are in keeping with this sense of the word, for she states that prayer expands her soul and unites her to Jesus. These seem to belong to the higher gifts, which Teresa calls *gustos* (God-given consolations). Indeed Teresa says that these expand the heart, which is equivalent to Thérèse's 'expand my soul'.[14]

Thérèse now seems to diverge as she speaks about prayers that were said in common. Each community had special prayers, and some of these were doubtless what Thérèse has just called 'beautiful'. Carmelite monasteries also had hermitages, places for special prayer for the nuns; these were in the garden, or in a specific part of the house. In Lisieux they were dedicated to the Sacred Heart, the Holy Face and St Joseph. Thérèse liked the prayers said in them; she says them with devotion, for she feels that the other sisters' fervour may make up for her deficiencies *(la ferveur de soeurs supplée à la mienne)*. It is not easy to tie down precisely what she means by the two words 'fervour' and 'devotion', which she uses in this passage. But it is worthwhile to attempt to grasp their meaning. They are not distinct, for the two words seem to indicate a prayer that is focused and is affective, that is, felt to be from the heart. She states that devotion is lacking when she says the rosary alone. She characterises this as an inability to concentrate on the mysteries *(je n'arrive pas à fixer mon esprit)*. What surprises her is that she loves the Blessed Virgin deeply, but cannot have devotion in saying a prayer to her (the rosary). Thérèse then takes consolation from the fact that Mary sees her good will. Hence we can deduce that prayer without devotion can mean prayer that is distracted, but offered with love and with the intention of praying. Here, as always, Thérèse gives the highest priority to love.

When she uses the word 'fervent' elsewhere, it indicates a prayer that is sincere and poured out from the depths of her being. Thus, at the cathedral before she met the bishop who could allow her to enter Carmel at fifteen; at the shrine of Our Lady of Victories; at the death of the saintly foundress of the Lisieux Carmel, Mother Geneviève de Saint Thérèse; in preparation for a retreat that was to be decisive for her growth – on these occasions she described herself as praying with great fervour.[15]

Many people will echo Thérèse's experience of difficulty with the rosary. One hears the difficulty expressed in the question: 'should one concentrate on the Hail Mary or on the mystery?' Experience shows that the solution does not lie in a simple choice of one or the other. The key to the rosary prayer lies somehow in our bringing an attitude of praise and worship to our insertion into the mysteries of Christ. It is, moreover, more important to enter with love into the infancy, passion and glorification of Jesus and Mary than to be overly concerned about the specifics of a mystery. In the end we should say the rosary as we can, not as we can't. As it is a prayer for sinners and mystics, each person can find an appropriate way of saying it, even if problems may be encountered in its recitation. From Thérèse we can, however, learn to be at peace about this prayer. Pope Paul VI perhaps goes even further as he writes:

> We desire that very worthy devotion should not be propagated in a way that is too one-sided or exclusive. The rosary is an excellent prayer, but the faithful should feel serenely free in its regard. They should be drawn to its calm recitation by its intrinsic appeal.[16]

Following both Paul VI and Thérèse, we can thus avoid unease or guilt about this prayer, which is so simple, yet at times apparently so formidable.

At the end of the passage that we have called her treatise on prayer, Thérèse moves from her difficulty in reciting the rosary to a broader issue of aridity. We should not confuse aridity with Thérèse's eighteen-month long trial of faith, which was characterised by a profound sense of absence of heaven. She described it as a dark tunnel, a wall reaching to the skies, which came between her and any reassuring sense of faith. It lasted, with a few brief intermissions, from Easter 1896 until the day she died, 30 September 1897.[17]

Thérèse does not refer to aridity very often in her writings; there are only about ten references to it. However, we know that aridity was her more or less constant state. Mother Agnes, her sister and prioress, testified at the beatification process:

> All her life she suffered aridity *(des aridités)*. When the distress increased, the reading of spiritual authors left her in aridity, but the Holy Gospel which she carried on her heart then filled her mind *(occupait alors son esprit)* and nourished her soul.[18]

Her sister Céline, Sr Geneviève, stated at the process that the greatest trials Thérèse suffered were an almost uninterrupted state of aridity in prayer, a lack of consideration by some other sisters who gave her left-overs at table and what Céline delicately refers to as the 'defective administration of Mother Gonzague whose unstable and bizarre character caused a lot of suffering to the sisters.'[19] Her references to aridity are not sufficiently explicit to enable us to tie down exactly the meaning of the word. But since the word has a long history, one can look at the generally understood meaning in the classical modern authors on the spiritual life.[20] Those in the tradition of St Ignatius will distinguish between aridity and desolation. The latter is characterised by sadness, weariness and anxiety and can constitute a tug away from God. Unlike desolation, which can affect the whole of the spiritual life, aridity is confined to prayer. Aridity ('dryness') is much more a certain powerlessness during prayer to elicit thoughts or affections about spiritual things. This powerlessness can be the fault of the person praying, perhaps some infidelity, serious resistance to grace, general tepidity or lukewarmness in serving God. It may also come from circumstances, such as external worries, physical or psychological weakness, or it may be a trial sent by God that purifies and strengthens the person. Dryness in practice is the absence of what makes prayer easy, so that, despite efforts, there is no longer any relish in prayer. One cannot surface appropriate thoughts; one experiences being empty or void during prayer. If one knows the reason for this problem and can do something about its causes, then it may be relieved. In many cases it just comes, and the only remedy is to remain faithful to the times of prayer. Such dryness is absolutely necessary for spiritual growth. When it is nice to pray, we may only be pleasing ourselves and enjoying the satisfaction we obtain. It is when prayer becomes dry and even almost impossible that our love is purified and we pray not for our own satisfaction but for God.

If one asks: how may the time of prayer be 'put in?' then Thérèse is immediately helpful. She clearly knows an aridity that comes from God and for which she is not to blame. She describes it with great accuracy: 'when my mind is in such aridity that it is impossible to draw from it one single thought to unite me with God.' She immediately adds how she prays:

> I very slowly recite an 'Our Father' and then the angelic salutation [the 'Hail Mary']; then these prayers give me great delight; they nourish my soul much more than if I had recited them precipitately a hundred times.[21]

Again, it is not difficult to see the influence of St Teresa of Avila here. When she was teaching her sisters of the Spanish Reform, books on prayer were generally unavailable; Church authorities had them put on the *Index*. She wrote: 'Hold fast, daughters, for they cannot take from you the 'Our Father' and the 'Hail Mary'.'[22] She wrote an extensive commentary on the 'Our Father',[23] and intended to write one on the 'Hail Mary' also. She proposes that the 'Our Father' be said with care:

> To recite the Our Father or the Hail Mary or whatever prayer you wish is vocal prayer. But behold what poor music you produce when you do this without mental prayer. Even the words will be poorly produced at times.[24]

Here, as in her daughter Thérèse, we see how easily vocal prayer and mental prayer blend together.

Thérèse then says that these prayers give her great delight and nourish her soul. We should not think, however, that slow devout recitation of these prayers would always banish aridity for Thérèse or anybody else. She makes the point clearer in another passage in which she speaks about aridity:

> Just as all those that followed it, my Profession retreat was one of great aridity. God showed me *clearly*, however, without my perceiving it, the way to please Him and to practise the most sublime virtues. I have frequently noticed that Jesus does not want me to lay up *provisions;* He nourishes me at each moment with totally new food; I find it within me without my knowing how it is there. I believe it is Jesus Himself hidden in the depths of my poor little heart: He is giving me the grace of acting within me, making me think of all He desires me to do at the present moment.[25]

Thérèse does not find ease in prayer, yet she is not without direction or appropriate guidance. She feels that the Lord places within her whatever she needs. Though she does not use the term 'infused knowledge', some form of divine communication is involved here.

A key to Thérèse's teaching on aridity, indeed of her whole view of prayer, is to be found in a letter written to Céline in July 1889. The context is important. In January of that year Thérèse received the Carmelite habit. Soon afterwards her father was placed in a mental hospital in Caen, where he would remain for three years. Thérèse poured out her soul to Céline, writing profound letters on suffering to her between February and April.[26] In this July letter, Thérèse is again opening her heart to Céline. The letter seems fragmentary with even more ellipsis points than usual:

> My soul doesn't leave you . . . it suffers with you! . . . Oh! how hard it is to live, to remain on this earth of bitterness and anguish. . . . But tomorrow . . . in an hour, we shall be at port, what joy! Ah, what a good it will be to contemplate Jesus *face to face* all through the *whole* of eternity! [...] What has Jesus done, then, to detach our souls from all that is created? Ah, He

has struck a great blow . . . but it is a blow of love. God is admirable, but He is especially loveable; let us love Him then. . . . let us love Him enough to suffer for Him all that He wills, even spiritual pains, aridities, anxieties, apparent coldness. . . . Ah! Here is great love, to love Jesus without feeling the sweetness of this love . . . this is martyrdom . . . Well, then, *let us die as martyrs*. Oh! Céline . . . sweet echo of my soul, do you understand . . . Unknown martyrdom, known to God alone [...] That is love pushed to the point of heroism.[27]

Despite its hesitant form, this letter shows astonishing maturity; Thérèse was all of sixteen when she wrote it. Both she and the whole family were in deep distress at the time. It is hard to imagine a greater trial for a French bourgeois family than to have their father committed to an asylum after some behaviour that was both outlandish and public. Thérèse admits to the distress, but looks through and beyond it to the Lord's love that is purifying them. Here we see that Thérèse avoids any selfish expression: it is the Lord's will that is paramount. She is, as always, a faithful daughter of the great Teresa, who wrote:

Don't think that in what concerns perfection there is some mystery or things unknown or still to be understood, for in perfect conformity to God's will lies all our good.[28]

In aridity, and in all her prayer, what matters is not Thérèse, but the opportunity for her to love.

This approach to aridity in prayer can remind us of her image of the little ball of Jesus. She first seems to have used it in a letter to her sister Pauline as she recounted what seems to have been the disaster of the papal audience; she seemed to have got nowhere with her direct appeal to the pope to enter Carmel at fifteen. She wrote:

God cannot give me trials that are above my strength. He has given me the courage to bear this trial. Oh! It is very great. . . . But, Pauline, I am the Child Jesus' little ball; if He wishes to break His toy, He is free. Yes, I will do all that He wills.[29]

She uses the same image when, about eight years later, she recalls these events in her life-story. She had offered herself to Jesus as his little toy to be treated as he pleased. Now He had apparently abandoned her and gone to sleep. But even if the little ball was sad to be left aside, she felt content as she was pleasing Jesus.[30] One could easily pass these passages by with their images of infancy – toys and little balls – without noticing the hard, uncompromising spirituality that lies beneath them. Here Thérèse is expressing not only her total abandonment to God, but also his acceptance of this offering.

Similarly, the little treatise on prayer that we have been examining is totally devoid of any focus on Thérèse. In prayer she considers only her Lord. We find the same outgoing love in the prayers that she wrote for herself and for others.

Prayers written by Thérèse

We have already seen that in her writings Thérèse moves easily from narrative to prayer. And so we find many short prayers scattered throughout her works. Moreover, the majority (thirty-three) of her sixty poems are actually prayers. But there is a special quality in twenty-one of these prayers, which have been gathered from her writings. The first is a thirteen-word plea to Mary: 'O my good Blessed Virgin, grant that your little Thérèse may stop tormenting herself.'[31] Thérèse is thirteen and publicity about her miraculous cure through the smile of the Virgin had led to deep distress, as she even began to wonder whether she had imagined the whole thing. She would be set free from this torment only three years later at the shrine of Our Lady of Victories on her way to Rome in 1887.[32] This prayer is direct and confident. Her last prayer, again to Mary, was written just three weeks before her death with great difficulty on the feast of the Birthday of Mary. It may seem at first sight difficult and rather complex:

> O Mary, if I were Queen of Heaven and you were Thérèse, I would want to be Thérèse so that you might be the Queen of Heaven!!!...............[33]

The three exclamation marks and the fifteen points were the last thing she would write. Scholars point out that in spiritual books of the time a sentence like this was found in which St Augustine of Hippo was said to have addressed a similar desire, but in his case it was to the Lord rather than to Mary.[34] Thérèse is here attempting to express her union of heart with Mary and her total self-giving to her.

Between the first and last prayers of Thérèse we find various kinds, depending on the intended recipients and the circumstances. Bishop G. Gaucher divides them into three: spontaneous prayers written in distress or in joy; 'pedagogical' prayers written for others, mostly novices; the four major prayers at decisive moments – her profession, act of oblation, a prayer for her spiritual brother and her consecration to the Holy Face of Jesus.[35]

In the prayers that she wrote for both herself and others we find common themes from the spirituality of the time. One idea that is particularly strong is Thérèse's appropriation of the merits of Jesus and of Mary and of the saints so as to offer them to the Father in intercession or reparation. Thérèse has nothing of her own; all that is of value already belongs to God. We can look at a short prayer, a morning offering, that she was asked to write for a lay friend of one of the Lisieux sisters:

> My God, I offer you all that I do today for the intentions and the glory of the Sacred Heart of Jesus. I want to sanctify every beat of my heart, my thoughts and my simplest works by uniting them to his infinite merits. I want to repair for my faults *(réparer mes fautes)* by casting them into the furnace of his merciful love. O my God! I ask you for myself and those dear to me the grace to fulfil perfectly your holy will and to accept for love of you the joys and sorrows of this passing life so that one day we may be reunited in Heaven for all eternity. Amen.[36]

Here in addition to the common themes of the traditional Morning Offering, we find typical Thérèse motifs – union with the merits of Christ, complete trust in divine mercy and perfect abandonment to the will of God.

We have noted what might be called the four great prayers of Thérèse, the prayers that bring us to the core of her spirituality. The first is her profession offering from 8 September 1890. Already the seventeen-year-old Thérèse has come into the heart of her vocation. There is nothing selfish in this prayer. She offers herself totally to God. She fears only sin. Apart from the gift of loving for herself she asks only for others. The heart of the prayer lies towards the end and in a final sentence:

> May your will be done in me perfectly, and may I arrive at the place you have prepared for me. [...] I want only to give you joy and console you.[37]

The second of the great prayers is the Act of Oblation to Merciful Love, which she made on Trinity Sunday, 9 June 1885 is one of the most sublime writings of Thérèse. It has often been studied and an adequate commentary is beyond the limits of this present work.[38] It is a lofty summary of her spirituality and represents a deepened grasp of the Little Way she had discovered that eight months earlier. The third prayer, 'Consecration to the Holy Face', was written by Thérèse for 6 August 1896, the Feast of the Transfiguration. She and two others initially made this act. These sisters, Geneviève of St Thérèse-Marie (Céline) and Marie of the Trinity had added to their names, 'of the Holy Face,' as had Thérèse on her profession day. It is prefaced by one of Thérèse's favourite quotations from St John of the Cross: 'For a little of this pure love is more beneficial to the Church than all these other works put together.'[39] Thérèse, her father and sisters had been members of the Confraternity of the Holy Face since 1885. Her father's illness and the fact that he literally went about with his face covered led to Thérèse having deeper insights into the Holy Face of Jesus.[40] The prayer of consecration takes up many of the themes of Thérèse. The focus is on their reciprocal love for Jesus, on his sufferings and on their desire to make reparation for the sins of others and to bring them salvation.

The fourth of the great prayers written by Thérèse is one she wrote almost immediately after receiving the task of spiritually caring for a future missionary, the Abbé Maurice Bellière, whom she will henceforth regard as her missionary brother.[41] Thérèse's prayer for him dates from October 1895, five months after the Act to Merciful Love. In it we can see the great themes of Thérèse's maturity. She begins by expressing her delight in having a missionary brother and in the grace of working in a particular way for one who would one day be a priest. She recognises her inadequacy, but says, 'You know, Lord, that my only ambition is to make you known and loved.' She likens herself to Moses, who prayed on a mountain for his people who were in battle (see Exodus 17:8–13); she prayed on Carmel, whilst her brother will fight in the plain. The military symbolism was dear to her from the Carmelite *Rule,* which has a long section devoted to the spiritual armour with which the Carmelite goes to battle against evil.[42] In the second half of the prayer she goes on to make direct intercession for him:

> Divine Jesus, hear the prayer I offer you for him who wants to be your Missionary. Keep him safe amid the dangers of the world. Make him feel increasingly the nothingness and vanity of passing things and the happiness of being able to despise them for your love. May he carry out his sublime apostolate on those around him. May he be an apostle worthy of your Sacred Heart. . . . O Mary! Gentle queen of Carmel, it is to you that I entrust the soul of the future priest whose unworthy little sister I am. Teach him even now how lovingly you handled the Divine Child Jesus and wrapped him in swaddling clothes, so that one day he may go up to the Holy Altar and carry in his hands the king of Heaven. I ask you also to keep him safe beneath the shadow of your virginal mantle until the happy day when he leaves this valley of tears and can contemplate your splendour and enjoy for all eternity the fruits of his glorious apostolate.[43]

In this prayer we see the directness of Thérèse. Without embellishment she goes to the heart of the missionary vocation as she perceives it. She knows of the dangers ahead of him; indeed the dangers and vanity of the world would later be a cause of great tension in his life. Her straightforward prayer to Mary takes up an idea found elsewhere in her writings – the comparison between Mary who physically cared for Jesus and the priest who handles the sacred Host. She is of course also suggesting to Maurice that he place himself under the care of Mary.

Conclusion

As we look at the range of prayers written by Thérèse as well as at her difficulties with vocal prayer, we can see one underlying principle. Whatever our prayer may be, it is our reaching to God that counts much more than the actual form or words. Moreover, what counts is not so much what is said, or even the mental intention that one manages to give to vocal prayer, but rather the love with which we are responding to God.

8

Thérèse Still Guides Us

We have, however briefly, sought to see what Thérèse had to say about prayer and how she prayed. One can see that much of this teaching is perennial in the sense that it would be appropriate for any time. One can wonder though if it might not have a special relevance for our age. We can look at some trends in our world and in the Church and find perhaps a special role for the teaching of Thérèse at the present moment.

Thérèse as a counter to modern ideologies

In the socio-economic North, that is, the rich and developed countries, including Australia, there are three dominant ideologies, which are negative. Ideologies of their very nature are exceedingly hard to pin down, but, once we become aware of one, we find it as an underlying assumption in the media, in entertainment, in business and in social relationships.

The first ideology, or widely held idea, is that of modern omniscience. More and more we know what earlier generations did not know. It is presumed that knowledge is an unquestioned good. It is implied that if we do not know everything now, one day we will. And with knowledge comes power. So the second ideology is omnipotence: science and technology have done so much, and eventually all problems will be solved. But even as science triumphs, doubts have already set in and the post-modernist approach finds the world not at all so logical and controllable as people recently assumed.

The third ideology has various characteristics, but is not easy to pin down clearly. Some people would call it the liberal agenda – minimum restraints, maximum freedom and a primary focus on the individual and personal gratification. We find in it also a typical mark of immaturity: gratification is not to be postponed. What is immediately painful is avoided and what is here and now pleasurable is sought.

The life and teaching of Thérèse stand as a rebuke to these ideologies of our time; rather than seek to know everything or accomplish everything, she sought to be little; instead of putting herself and her own needs first, she put God first and loved her companions without self-seeking.

One can make a good case for saying that all sin is selfishness; if that be so, then prayer is a sure antidote. In prayer we admit that we are no longer the centre of our own world. No matter how limited or inadequate a prayer might be, it is, at the very least, an admission that we are in need and that God can come to our aid. When we move from self-centred to God-centred praying, such as thanksgiving and praise, we find meaning and truth for others and ourselves.

In the very last pages of her life-story, Thérèse ponders the age-old tension between Martha and Mary (see Luke 10:38–42). At this stage she is already so weak that she writes in pencil. She defends Martha's role; did not the Mother of Jesus prepare meals for the Holy Family? It was the restlessness *(inquiétude)* of Martha that earned the Lord's rebuke. Her thoughts then open out into a vision of the vocation of Martha's sister, Mary:

> All the saints have understood this, and more especially those who filled the world with the light of the gospel teachings. Was it not in prayer *(oraison)* that St Paul, St Augustine, St John of the Cross, St Thomas Aquinas, St Francis, St Dominic, and so many other famous Friends of God have drawn out this divine science which delights the greatest geniuses? A scholar has said, *'Give me a lever and a fulcrum and I will lift the world.'* What Archimedes was not able to obtain, for this request was not directed by God and was only made from a material viewpoint, the saints have obtained in all its fullness. The Almighty has given them as fulcrum: *Himself alone (Lui-même, et Lui seul)*. As lever: prayer which sets alight a fire of love *(l'oraison qui embrase d'un feu d'amour)*. And it is in this way

that they have lifted the world; it is in this way that the saints still on earth *(les Saints encore militants)* lift it, and that, until the end of time, the saints to come will lift it.[1]

Thérèse was fascinated by the science she studied, and she uses examples from it to great effect in her works. Here she recalls the idea of the lever, which when it rests on a support or fulcrum can be used to lift much greater loads than a person could with sheer brute strength. It is at this point that Thérèse is at her most counter-cultural and in opposition to the ideologies mentioned above. She sees the key to the transformation of the world as lying not in knowledge and power, much less in selfishness, but in prayer, which as an all-powerful lever is resting on God alone as fulcrum. Even more the prayer she refers to is not just any prayer, but one 'which sets alight a fire of love' (these words were added later by Thérèse).

A complex world with many problems is brought to God in prayer and love. Even though we may lack the total dedication of Thérèse we can still make a difference to a world in distress as we apply her lever and fulcrum in our celebration of the Eucharist; there we genuinely enter into the transformation of the world.

A recent study has looked at the desolation of Thérèse at the end of her life, her trial of faith referred to earlier.[2] Its author, Mary Frohlich, suggests that Thérèse can be seen as in solidarity with all who have lost a sense of meaning in some night of nothingness, and for whom the traditional presentations of faith no longer appeal. In the darkness that enveloped her she held on to faith and still continued to lay down her life for others in the Church. Less than three months before she died she said:

> I can't think very much about the happiness of heaven; only one expectation makes my heart beat, and it is the love that I shall receive and I shall be able to give. And then I think of all the good I would like to do after my death: have little children baptised, help priests, missionaries, the whole Church.[3]

And in that darkness she continued to pray. The way she prayed has important lessons for our time.

An enduring tension

In spirituality there are two errors that are at two quite opposite poles, Pelagianism and Quietism. Both are heresies and totally destructive of the spiritual life. Pelagianism, called after a British theologian who taught in Rome in the late fourth century, over-emphasises the human effort, and does not allow for the necessity of grace. Quietism, a movement in seventeenth-century French spirituality, relies on God in such a way that human activity and responsibility are excessively diminished. Whilst none of us is likely to be a Pelagian or Quietist in a pure or heretical form, we can very easily veer too much in either direction. The spirituality of Thérèse stands against these twin dangers of exaggerated self-reliance and passivity. Some of her finest theology lies in the letter she wrote for her sister Marie, explaining what God had done for her. She asks 'How can a soul as imperfect as mine aspire to the possession of the plenitude of *Love?'*[4] Her answer unfolds in the parable of a little bird. The apparent artlessness of this parable hides profound doctrine.[5] She is the little bird and Jesus is both the sun, which she seeks, and the divine eagle, with whose wings she can fly. At another level the little bird is contrasted with the great eagles, the saints who can fly right up to the furnace of the Trinity. She states her desire to fly like them, and concludes: 'But alas! The only thing it can do is *raise its little wings;* to fly is not within its *little* power!'[6] As she develops the parable, it becomes even clearer that Thérèse, the little bird, cannot undertake anything great. But she does what she can: she raises her wings, keeps gazing at the Sun, confesses her weakness, accepting in peace any apparent neglect on the part of the eagle. She is neither completely passive, nor foolishly self-reliant. She then develops in another way the theme of littleness:

> Jesus, I am too little to perform great actions, and my own *folly* is this: to trust that Your Love will accept me as a victim. My *folly* consists in begging the eagles my brothers, to obtain for me the favour of flying towards the Sun of Love with the Divine Eagle's own wings. As long as You desire it, O my Beloved, Your little bird will remain without strength and without wings, and will always stay with its gaze fixed on You.[7]

We can clearly see the spiritual balance of Thérèse here, and how she avoids both extremes of Pelagianism and Quietism. There would, however, seem to be those who misinterpreted her works. The French are very wary of Quietism, an error that had deceived some of the finest spiritual writers of the seventeenth-century. Her sister Céline (Sr Geneviève) took up this charge when she collected her memories of Thérèse. Céline refuted any such accusation in a text that brings us in a simple way to the heart of Thérèse's doctrine:

> Although her *Little Way, the Way of Spiritual Childhood,* is a way of complete confidence, Thérèse was far from minimising the role of personal co-operation in the matter of our salvation. She was always emphasising this point in her instructions to us in the novitiate. There could be no better proof of the importance she attached to this idea than the example of her own spiritual life: it was one long series of generous and consistent acts of virtue.
>
> I had been struck by the passage in *Ecclesiasticus,* 'All mercy shall make a place for every man according to the merits of his works and according to the wisdom of his sojournment' (Eccl 16:15 from the Latin Vulgate). Discussing this with Thérèse I said that I thought she had directed the course of her life with a wisdom that was sublime; consequently, a very special place must be reserved in heaven for her. The phrase 'according to his works,' however bothered me.
>
> Spiritedly Thérèse explained that confidence in God and the virtue of abandonment are nourished only by sacrifice. 'We must do all in our power,' she said, 'to give without counting and to deny ourselves constantly. We must prove our love by all the good works of which we are capable and which, after all, are of little worth . . . Even when we have done all that we think should be done, we are to consider ourselves 'unprofitable servants' (Luke 17:10), hoping at the same time that God will, through His grace, give us all that we desire. This is what all little souls who 'run' in the way of spiritual childhood should hope for.' 'Remember,' she reminded me, 'I say "run," not "rest"'.[8]

Here we see perfect spiritual equilibrium: Thérèse avoids Quietism by insisting on human effort; she avoids Pelagianism by remembering that all is under grace. There are other significant ways in which she is also a sure guide.

Thérèse and spiritual guidance

When we survey Thérèse's writings we can be struck by the depth of wisdom that they contain. We might wonder where she got it, who guided her. But in fact she did not receive very much guidance, she had no spiritual director in any practical sense, even though she did meet and had some extensive correspondence with her sister Céline's director, the Jesuit Fr Almire Pichon. She did not see him after November 1888 when he was assigned to Canada. He wrote to her until 1895. On at least one occasion he advised her when her problem of scrupulosity threatened to recur. Various priests in confession or in homilies said things that she found helpful. But her ongoing direction was mainly what she received from the scriptures and in her prayer. Indeed she stated late in her life: 'I understand and I know from experience that: "The kingdom of God is within you" (Luke 17:21). Jesus has no need of books or teachers to instruct souls; he teaches without the noise of words.'[9]

Thérèse goes further and says several times that Jesus alone was her director.[10] Writing to Céline in the summer of 1893 she talks about spiritual directors and Jesus in a way that anticipates the Little Way, which she would articulate fully only fifteen months later:

> Directors have others advance in perfection by having them perform a great number of acts of virtue, and they are right; but my director, who is Jesus, teaches me not to count up my acts. He teaches me to do *all* through love, to refuse Him nothing, to be content when He gives me a chance of proving to Him that I love Him. But this is done in peace, in *abandonment*, it is Jesus who is doing all in me, and I am doing nothing.[11]

Here we see again the tension between what God does, *all*, and what Thérèse does, which is paradoxically likewise *all*. It is also the first time the word 'abandonment' appears in her letters.

One of the central points made by Pope John Paul II in declaring
Thérèse a doctor of the Church was what he called 'her special
charism of wisdom'.[12] If the pope is using the word 'charism' in a
technical sense – and given the solemnity of the document he
probably is – then he is asserting that the wisdom that she received
was primarily for others, for the Church.[13] As well as being mainly for
others, another mark of charism is that it is from the Holy Spirit.

We ought not, however, to think of Thérèse as being only, or even
primarily, enlightened by the Spirit within. Not many Christians, or
even religious, have a specialist spiritual director. But all need
direction. Such direction comes from the scriptures, the liturgy, talks
and sermons, books, casual conversations with friends and relatives,
the knockabout of life itself. One can suggest rather more. Some
theologians would see the deepest meaning of the Church being
apostolic, in that God ordained that we are to be saved not directly,
but through others,[14] Thérèse was very aware that God used her to
guide other people, both her novices[15] and especially her missionary
brothers. Their first thought was more or less to have a nun to pray
for them. Thérèse did this, but she moved very quickly to be their
spiritual friend, indeed their guide. Her letters are strong, at times
stern, but always loving calls to holiness. She genuinely hoped that
they would be martyrs! She invited them to nothing less than she
herself had discovered – total abandonment to God and confidence
in his mercy and love.[16]

Within the convent she had a great influence on her novices,
whom she led with kindness and firmness. Whilst she could
understand frailty and weakness, she never ceased to present the
highest ideals. So it is not surprising that she shared her insights into
the Holy Face of Jesus with her novices. As we saw in the previous
chapter, all three of them signed the Consecration to the Holy Face
in 1896.[17]

Her eagerness to share the gifts she received is even clearer in the
case of her Act of Oblation to Merciful Love.[18] In spirituality at that
time, offering as victims to God for others were quite common.
Though she admired its generosity, Thérèse was not at all attracted to
the idea of offering herself as a victim of divine justice. She felt deeply
drawn to God's mercy and love.[19] She composed an Act of Oblation

to Merciful Love, which represents one of the peaks of her spiritual journey and might be considered as a major text in the history of spirituality.[20] In it we find all the main themes of her spirituality, especially her Little Way, her deep sense of Church, and a profound intuition of the meaning of divine mercy and love. Thérèse made the oblation on Trinity Sunday, 9 June 1895. Almost immediately she shared this with her sister Céline. Having obtained permission from their sister, Mother Agnes, who really did not understand it very well, Thérèse and Céline made the act together two days later before the statue of Our Lady, which had smiled on Thérèse and saved her life when she was in danger of death in May 1883. She next spoke of the offering with her sister Marie who, after some hesitation, offered herself that same summer of 1895.[21] Then Thérèse brought it to the notice of her novice, the generous-spirited Marie of the Trinity, who, again after hesitation, made the offering in December. Her sister Pauline, Mother Agnes, was somewhat embarrassed by the fact that she adopted the oblation only much later.[22] Given the fact that Agnes was both her sister and her superior, Thérèse may not have been as forceful or persuasive in her case. Thérèse did, however, speak about the oblation several times in the *Last Conversations*.[23]

There is a very strong conclusion to that part of her *Story of a Soul*, which was a letter Thérèse wrote to her sister Marie:

> O Jesus! Why can't I tell all *little souls* how unspeakable is Your condescension? I feel that if You found a soul weaker and littler than mine, which is impossible, You would be pleased to grant it still greater favours, provided it abandoned itself with total confidence to Your Infinite Mercy. But why do I desire to communicate Your secrets of love, O Jesus, for was it not You alone who taught them to me, and can You not reveal them to others? Yes, I know it, and I beg You to do it. I beg You to cast Your Divine Glance upon a great number of *little* souls. I beg You to choose a legion of *little* Victims worthy of Your LOVE![24]

Here at the end of the letter we find what the editor of the recent critical edition of the autobiography, Conrad De Meester, calls 'a short brief synthetic evocation of the Little Way'.[25] It is all there:

littleness, confidence, abandonment to divine mercy, love. In the above passage there is something of a missionary spirit. It is found even more clearly in the text when she expressed her deepest desires: 'Ah! in spirit of my littleness, I would like to enlighten souls as did the *Prophets* and the *Doctors*.'[26] Quite simply, she wished others also to have what she received.

Many are called
In the writings of Thérèse we find some hints of a question that has been tantalising in the Carmelite tradition: Why do so few seem to reach the heights of holiness? This issue is particularly important for Carmelites in view of the famous statement about the two aims of the Order in *The Institute of the First Monks*. St Teresa of Avila and St John of the Cross regarded this as a document dating long before the *Rule*, perhaps as early as the sixth century. Modern scholarship, however, assigns it to the fourteenth century. Using the image of the prophet Elijah hiding by the brook (1 Kgs 17:3–5) The *Institutes* stated:

> In regard to that life we may distinguish two aims, the one of which we may attain to, with the help of God's grace, by our own efforts and by virtuous living. This is to offer God a heart holy and pure from all actual stain of sin. This we achieve when we become perfect and hidden in Cherith (see 1 Kgs 17:2–4) – that is in charity [. . .] The other aim of this life is something that can be bestowed upon us only by God's bounty: namely to taste in our hearts and experience in our minds, not only after death but even during this mortal life, something of the power of the divine presence, and the bliss of heavenly glory.[27]

In view of the fact that Carmelites are thus encouraged to aim at the mystical life, both Teresa and John wonder why there are not more arriving at it. In the Prologue to the *Ascent of Mount Carmel* John indicates that lack of generosity and submission may be to blame, but he reserves his strongest censures for spiritual directors, which at the time mostly meant confessors. They kept people back through their ignorance.[28]

Teresa of Avila comes back to the matter several times, for example in speaking of what she calls 'the prayer of quiet', which begins the mystical life: 'I know many souls that reach this stage but to me it is a terrible pity that those that pass beyond, as they should, are so few I am ashamed to mention it.' She goes on to state her belief that there must be many,[29] but she, the Reformer of Carmel, does not know them.

For our time there would seem to be two answers to this problem about why so few seem to advance. One is that of Karl Rahner, who stresses what he calls 'the mysticism of everyday life'. Rahner is opposed to any elitist ideas about mysticism and holds that many people have genuine mystical experiences. Indeed he says memorably, 'The Christian of the future will be a mystic or he will not exist at all.'[30] Thus we can answer, with Rahner, that there are indeed many mystics, but we have misunderstood where mysticism is to be found, that is, in the challenges of life.

The other answer is that of Thérèse. She too is convinced that God wills to bring many to profound holiness. She exclaims 'Ah! how many souls would have reached sanctity had they been well directed.'[31] But for Thérèse good direction lies in teaching people the way of littleness, of being open to God's mercy through confidence and trust.

A teacher for our time

Earlier in this chapter we noted three ideologies of our time and suggested that the life and mission of Thérèse formed an important counter to these dominant ideas in our own culture. There is yet another, very destructive philosophy that we call 'pragmatism'. It includes a variety of notions that suggest that we must be efficient, that what does not seem to produce results is irrelevant, if not harmful, that people are to be valued by what they do and contribute rather than by what they are.

Prayer is not obviously a productive activity. Though it does bear fruits, we cannot always gauge them. Prayer is about a relationship between God and us. It both expresses and forms this relationship.

We have already spoken about Thérèse and prayer in earlier chapters. We now need to see how we can learn from her and from the Great Teresa about the way in which prayer affects our Christian living.

It is worthwhile considering for a moment what Teresa of Avila, from whom the Lisieux Carmelite learned so much, had to say about prayer. Teresa is teaching her sisters about prayer and she gives what underlies all her teaching. To the question: how to pray? she answers, 'The important thing is not to think much but to love much.'[32] And to the question of how we may judge our prayer, she directs us to God's will and says: 'It is in the effects and deeds following afterward that one discerns the true value of prayer; there is no better crucible for testing prayer.'[33]

At the beginning, we raised the question of whether or not Thérèse might have a Little Way of prayer. In the event we saw not another method or way of praying, but the context in which we are to pray. It is simply the Little Way itself. On the side of God Thérèse sees love and mercy. On our side she proposes a littleness that is founded on confidence. She wrote a letter to her sister Marie, who was both delighted and depressed by what Thérèse had revealed about the graces she received.[34] Marie was filled with joy at what God had been doing in her youngest sister, but she felt that this grace was far beyond her own reach. Thérèse tries to reassure her eldest sister and gives what is, in fact, a commentary on the Little Way. In it she sums up her own insight: 'It is confidence and nothing but confidence that must lead us to Love.'[35]

It does not matter then at what stage of spiritual growth we may be, or what way of praying we may be engaged in at any particular time; it is rather the relationship that we have with God that is decisive. And for Thérèse this relationship is best expressed in the Little Way of confidence and love. In it we find an antidote to the modern glorification of efficiency and the accompanying demeaning of the human person. Praying with Thérèse involves taking seriously our supreme dignity as God's children and acting out this relationship in prayer; all of this leads to love. If God cares for us, as indeed he does, and we can have confidence in his mercy and love, then we are free to serve him and others with creativity and simplicity. In the end we return to a recurring theme: Thérèse would not so much encourage us to pray as to love; if we genuinely love, then we shall surely pray, and pray well. Thérèse could not conceive of a love that fails to pray to God with adoration and thanksgiving, and that would not bring others to his mercy. Her prayer, which stands opposed to modern pragmatism, is nonetheless supremely fruitful, for her vocation was to be 'love in the heart of the Church'.[36]

A guide for today

At the beginning of this book we posed the question of what might St Thérèse of Lisieux, the newly proclaimed doctor of the Church, have to offer people who are concerned with their prayer. In one sense it might seem strange in today's busy secular world to seek help from one who lived in enclosure, almost totally cut off even from her own world. The amount of time she spent in prayer each day – about six hours – would seem to place her outside any possibility of imitation. Her lifestyle and the *Rule* of Carmel facilitated a life of concentrated prayer. So can she really be a teacher of prayer for the Church at large today?

It is important that one uses an expression such as 'a teacher' since in the Church there are many teachers, and there is not one that can be called the best. In the subjective activity of praying, people will be drawn sometimes to one guide, sometimes to another. Rich and beautiful as the teaching of Thérèse undoubtedly is, it does not attract everybody. Some people, even the great Karl Rahner, found her language and culture a real barrier to appreciating her teaching. The good news, however, is that we do not have to be taught by Thérèse. If we do not find her attractive after several attempts, we should leave her aside, returning to her later, or perhaps never. There are plenty of other schools of spirituality and spiritual guides.

For those who are drawn to Thérèse it is not hard to see her as a contemporary guide. Not only did she encounter serious difficulty in prayer, but also her experience of the dark night of faith will resonate with many who struggle in the darkness of our world. They will still have to come to terms with the language of Thérèse and her symbols, which are clearly late nineteenth century and French. But the effort will be rewarding.

In looking at Thérèse as a guide, it is important to grasp what she has to offer. She does not teach so much a method of prayer as a way of praying. The way of praying is itself a way of life. Her Little Way of littleness before God in serene confidence of his merciful love is the attitude we can bring to prayer. Her teaching invites us to a change of mind and heart so that we can approach God. We may not at a particular time feel attracted to her Act of Oblation to Merciful Love, but her simplicity and trust are sure foundations for prayer. In the end what most counts is our relationship with God, responding to his love, which first calls us. All prayer – liturgical, personal or vocal – reaches out to God. Any and every prayer answers to Thérèse's description to which we have continually returned in this book and which expresses to God her deepest reality:

> For me, prayer is an aspiration of the heart, it is a simple glance directed to heaven, it is a cry of gratitude and love in the midst of trial as well as joy; finally it is something great, supernatural, which expands my soul and unites me to Jesus.[37]

$\mathcal{N}otes$

Chapter 1: A Teacher of Prayer

1   See D. J. Billy and D. L. Orsuto, eds., *Spirituality and Morality: Integrating Prayer and Action* (New York: Paulist Press, 1996), passim and esp. 68–78.

2   *The Ascent of Mount Carmel,* Prologue 6 in *The Collected Works of St John of the Cross,* trans. K. Kavanaugh and O. Rodriguez (Washington DC: Institute of Carmelite Studies, revised ed. 1991), 117.

3   See *The Interior Castle,* Prologue 1 and 4 in *The Collected Works of St Teresa of Avila.* 3 vols, trans. O. Rodriguez and K. Kavanaugh (Washington DC: Institute of Carmelite Studies, 1976-1985), 2:281, 282.

4   *Catechism of the Catholic Church,* # 2558 (Dublin: Veritas, 1994), 544.

5   Ibid. On prayer see ## 2558–2865, on liturgy ## 1135–1209, pp. 544-610 and 260-275.

6   SSoul ch. 11, 243/ Ms C–G 25r, OeuvC 268/CritEd 287.

7   See the concordance of Thérèse by Soeur Geneviève et al, *Les mots de sainte Thérèse de l'Enfant-Jésus et de la Sainte-Face* (Paris: Cerf, 1996).

8   See M.-Th. Aunis, 'Thérèse de Lisieux: De la prière à Jésus à la prière en Jésus', *Vie thérésienne* 25/97 (1985), 13–26; Bernard L. Gabriel, 'Vie d'oraison chez ste Thérèse de l'Enfant-Jésus', ibid. 27/106 (1987), 27–43; P. Bolognese, 'La preghiera è un semplice sguardo, uno slancio del cuore', *Rivista di vita spirituale* 43 (1989), 596–602; R. de Lima Gouvêa, 'La vie d'oraison chez sainte Thérèse de l'Enfant Jésus', *Près de la source* (Bourges) 42 (1997), 3–12; A. de Sutter, 'Pregare è sopratutto amare: Teresa di Gesù Bambino' in E. Ancili, *La preghiera: Bibbia, teologia, e esperienze storiche.* 2 vols. (Rome: Città Nuova, 1988), 1:397–415; A. de Sutter, 'La prière de sainte Thérèse de Lisieux', *Ephemerides carmeliticae* 24 (1973), 44–85; Fr Ivan, 'L'oraison de Thérèse', *Vives flammes* 222 (1996), 32–46; A. Riaud, 'Sainte Thérèse de l'Enfant-Jésus et la prière', *Les annales de sainte Thérèse de Lisieux,* 65/679–682 (1989), 11–13, 7–9, 13–15 and 8–10;

9   For example, articles by De Sutter (n. 8) and P. Teixeira Cavalcante, *Dicionário de santa Teresinha: Pequena enciclopédia sobre santa Teresinha* (São Paulo: Paulus, 1997), s.v. 'Oração', etc.

Chapter 2: A Life of Continual Prayer

1   For indications see biographies, for example, G. Gaucher, *The Story of a
     Life: St Thérèse of Lisieux* (San Francisco: HarperCollins, 1993), 1–84; C.
     de Meester, *Saint Thérèse of Lisieux: Her Life, Times and Teaching*
     (Washington DC: ICS, 1997); S.-J. Piat, *The Story of a Family: The Home
     of the Little Flower* (Dublin: Gill and Son, 1949), passim esp. ch. 11, pp.
     230–259.

2   SSoul ch. 2, 41–43/MS A 17r–18r, OeuvC 95–97/CritEd 101–103.

3   See SSoul ch. 1, 28–29/MS A 11r, OeuvC 85–86/CritEd 91.

4   SSoul ch. 4, 73–74/MS A 33r, OeuvC 121/CritEd 128–129.

5   March 1884, LT 11/Letters 1:190–191 with n. 3 – OeuvC 303.

6   SSoul ch. 1, 25/MS A 8v, OeuvC 82/CritEd 87.

7   SSoul ch. 1, 29/MS A 11r–v, OeuvC 86/CritEd 91–92.

8   SSoul ch. 4, 86/MS A 40r, OeuvC 133–134/CritEd 141.

9   SSoul ch. 2, 43/MS A 18r, OeuvC 97/CritEd 103.

10   SSoul ch. 1, 26–27/MS A 9v, OeuvC 83/CritEd 89.

11   See M. Baudouin-Croix, *Léonie Martin: A Difficult Life* (Dublin: Veritas,
     1993).

12   SSoul ch. 3, 57/MS A 25r–v, OeuvC 108/CritEd 114–115.

13   SSoul ch. 5, 104/MS A 48r, OeuvC 147–148/CritEd 155–157.

14   SSoul ch. 5, 106/MS A 49v, OeuvC 150/CritEd 159.

15   SSoul ch. 5, 106–107/MS A 49v, OeuvC 150/CritEd 159.

16   SSoul ch. 2, 37/MS A 14v, OeuvC 31/CritEd 97.

17   SSoul ch. 2, 43/MS A 18r, OeuvC 97/CritEd 102–103.

18   SSoul ch. 2, 48–49/MS A 21v–22r, OeuvC 102–103/CritEd 108–109.

19   SSoul ch. 6, 125–126/MS A 57v–58r, OeuvC 166–167/CritEd 175–176.

20   SSoul ch. 3, 54/MS A 23r, OeuvC 105/CritEd 111–112.

21   SSoul ch. 4, 81/MS A 37r, OeuvC 128/CritEd 135–136.

22   SSoul ch. 4, 76 and 71/MS A 34v and 31v, OeuvC 124, 119/CritEd 131,
     126.

23   SSoul ch. 5, 102/MS 47r, OeuvC 146/CritEd 153.

24   SSoul ch. 5, 102-103/MS A 47v, OeuvC 146/CritEd 154.

25   SSoul ch. 2, 38/MS A 15v, OeuvC 93/CritEd 98; for prayer see CritEd 98,
     n. 68 and Piat, op. cit. 184.

26   SSoul ch. 4, 71/MS A 31r, OeuvC 118/CritEd 125.

27   SSoul ch. 4, 74–75/MS A 33v, OeuvC 122/CritEd 129.

28   SSoul ch. 3, 53 and 81–82/MS A 22v and 37r, OeuvC 104, 129/CritEd
     111, 136.

29   SSoul ch. 5, 109/MS A 51r, OeuvC 153/CritEd 162.

30   SSoul ch. 10, 208/MS C–G 3r, OeuvC 237–238/CritEd 252–253.

31   SSoul ch. 10, 207–208/MS C–G 2r–3r, OeuvC 236–238/ CritEd
     251–253.

32 For example, Gaucher, op. cit. (n. 1) 138–140; De Meester, op. cit. (n. 1) 147–153.

33 SSoul ch. 8, 181/MS A 84r, OeuvC 212/CritEd 227.

Chapter Three: A Carmelite at Prayer

1 SSoul ch. 4, 80; ch. 8, 166–167/Ms A 36v; 76v, OeuvC 128; 199/CritEd 135; 209–210.

2 SSoul ch. 9, 195/Ms B–M 4r, OeuvC 227/CritEd 334 and PN 12:4/74,OeuvC 658.

3 SSoul ch. 9, 195/Ms B–M 3v, OeuvC 227/CritEd 333.

4 16 July 1896, LT 192/Letters 2:969, OeuvC 545.

5 For example, E. R. Carroll, 'Thérèse and the Mother of God', *Experiencing Saint Thérèse Today.* Carmelite Studies 5 (Washington: ICS, 1990), 82–96; M.-J. Nicolas, 'The Virgin Mary in the Gospel and in the Church according to St Teresa of Lisieux', *Sicut Parvuli* 19 (1957), 68–85, 116–125 [= *Revue thomiste* 52 (1952), 508–527]; R.M. Valabek, 'More Mother than Queen: Our Lady of Mount Carmel and St Teresa of Lisieux', *Carmel in the World* 20 (1981), 51–78; for references see C. O'Donnell, *Love in the Heart of the Church: The Mission of Thérèse of Lisieux* (Dublin: Veritas, 1997), 58–61 with nn. 7–23.

6 SSoul ch. 3, 65–66/Ms A 30r–v, OeuvC 116–117/CritEd 122–124.

7 SSoul ch. 6, 123/Ms A 56v–57r, OeuvC 164–165/CritEd 174–175.

8 PN 54/211–220, OeuvC 750–756.

9 LastConv 21.8.3/161–162, OeuvC 1102–1104.

10 SSoul ch. 3, 66/Ms A 30v, OeuvC 117/CritEd 124 and LT 182/Letters 2:929, OeuvC 527.

11 SSoul 278/Ms A 86, OeuvC 215/CritEd 231.

12 LastConv 30.9/204–206, OeuvC 1142–1147.

13 LT 114, 142, 165/Letters 1:662–663, 2:795, 861, OeuvC 420, 464, 498; see also SSoul ch. 5, 109; 6, 139/Ms A 51r and 66r, OeuvC 153, 180/CritEd 162, 190.

14 RP 6, OeuvC 898, 900, 908, 911, 912.

15 SSoul ch. 7, 148/Ms A 69v, OeuvC 186/CritEd 196; see in final poem of RP 6, 'The deserts will one day be re-peopled', OeuvC 912.

16 Soul ch. 3, 58/Ms A 26r, OeuvC 109/CritEd 116.

17 SSoul ch. 3, 57/Ms A 25v, OeuvC 109/CritEd 115.

18 For example SSoul ch. 6, 139/MS A 66r; OeuvC 180/CritEd 190; LT 36/Letters 1:354; LT 94/1:577; LT 139/2:765; LT 261/2:1165 (in French), OeuvC 329, 396, 455, 620; RP 1,14v,14; 3,7r,3; 3,7v,1; 3,8v,8, OeuvC 793, 826, 827; 829.

19 SSoul ch. 4, 73/Ms A 32v, OeuvC 121/CritEd 128.

20 SSoul ch. 4, 79/Ms A 36v, OeuvC 127/CritEd 134.

21   SSoul ch. 4, 84/Ms A 39r, OeuvC 132/CritEd 139.

22   LT 213/Letters 2:1041, OeuvC 569.

23   See SSoul ch. 7, 148/Ms A 69v, OeuvC 186/CritEd 196.

24   LT 182/Letters 2:926, OeuvC 523.

25   *Constitutions* 7 in *Complete Works* 3:320.

26   See commentaries on the *Rule*, for example the recent K. Waaijman, *The Mystical Space of Carmel: A Commentary on the Carmelite Rule* (Leuven: Peeters, 1999), 214–235.

27   For example 'Living on Love', PN 17, see LastConv 5,8,7/134, OeuvC 1078.

28   LastConv 6,8,5/137, OeuvC 1081.

29   LastConv 6.4.1/36, OeuvC 991.

30   For example SSoul ch. 8, 174/Ms A 81r, OeuvC 206/CritEd 219; ch. 9, 187/Ms B-M 1r, OeuvC 219/CritEd 324.

31   LT 220/Letters 2:1059, OeuvC 574.

32   LT 122/Letters 2:708, OeuvC 430.

33   PS 7:1–4/232, OeuvC 765. See also 'Silence is the language of the blessed inhabitants of heaven.' LT 163/Letters 2:853 with 854, n. 4, OeuvC 496 and 1322, n.3.

34   LT 163/Letters 2:853, OeuvC 496.

35   LT 145/Letters 2:808, OeuvC 470.

36   PN 13:13/78, OeuvC 661.

37   PN 24:5, 5–6/124, OeuvC 693.

38   PN 54: 8,5–8 and 24:1–8/216,220, OeuvC 752, 756.

39   LT 161/Letters 2:851, OeuvC 493.

40   LT 74/Letters 2:499, OeuvC 370.

41   PN 38:2,3–4 and 3,1–2.

42   *Spiritual Canticle,* St 14.

43   LT 135/Letters 2:752, OeuvC 448.

44   LT 138/Letters 2:764, OeuvC 454.

45   PN 21:3, 2-3/112, OeuvC 686.

Chapter Four: Liturgical Prayer

1   *Rule,* new numbering #11 (traditional chapter 8).

2   *Constitutions* 3 in *Collected Works,* trans. K. Kavanaugh and O. Rodriguez, 3 vols. (Washington: ICS, 1976–1985), 3:319. See also *On Making the Visitation* 30 in *Collected Works* 3:347.

3   See *Constitution on the Liturgy,* SC 88–99.

4   A. Bugnini, *The Reform of the Liturgy 1948–1975* (Collegeville: Liturgical Press, 1990), 522. The quotation continues: 'It is truly a theological, pastoral, ascetical and liturgical treatise on the prayer of the Hours, on the importance of this liturgy, and on its component parts. It

is a directory that serves not only for the celebration of the liturgy but for meditation on it.'

5   SSoul ch. 1, 26/Ms A 9v, OeuvC 83/CritEd 88.

6   SSoul ch. 2, 42/Ms A 17v, OeuvC 96/CritEd 102.

7   SSoul ch. 4, 75–76/Ms A 34r, OeuvC 123/CritEd 131.

8   SSoul ch. 11, 242/Ms C–G 25r, OeuvC 268/CritEd 287.

9   LT 182/Letters 2:932, OeuvC 528.

10   See LT 149/Letters 2:827-828, OeuvC 477–478

11   PN 24:14/126, OeuvC 695–696.

12   *Constitution on the Liturgy* SC 83 in A. Flannery, ed., *Vatican Council II: Constitution, Decrees, Declarations* (Northport NY: Costello – Dublin: Dominican Publications, revised ed. 1996), 144.

13   LastConv 18.5.4/45–46, OeuvC 999.

14   LastConv 12.6.1/63, OeuvC 1015; see also 12.8.4/147, OeuvC 1090.

15   LastConv 3.7.7/72–73, OeuvC 1023.

16   LastConv 6.8.6/137–138, OeuvC 1081.

17   Her sister Céline recalled: 'My sister's deep spirit of faith inspired her with great reverence for priests because of their sacerdotal dignity. She often expressed a certain regret at her own exclusion from the priesthood . . . [On hearing that a sister had brought the Blessed Sacrament miraculously to St Stanislaus Koska, Thérèse remarked] "What marvels shall we not behold in heaven! I truly believe that those who so lovingly desired the priesthood and have not attained it in this world will enjoy all its privileges in the next."' CS ch.4 118–119/ch. 4, 100.

18   PN 40:7–8/171, OeuvC 725,

19   LT 135/Letters 2:753, OeuvC 449.

20   *Constitutions*, chs. 11–12 in *Complete Works of St Teresa*, trans. E. Allison Peers, vol. 3 (London: Sheed and Ward, 1957), 232–233.

21   CS ch. 4, 103/ch. 3, 69.

22   CS ch. 4, 102/ch. 3, 68.

23   PA 267.

24   CS ch. 4 103/ch. 3, 69.

25   See C. O'Donnell, 'The Communion of Saints', *Love in the Heart of the Church: The Mission of St Thérèse of Lisieux* (Dublin: Veritas, 1997), 54–67.

26   See *La Bible avec Thérèse de Lisieux: Textes de saint Thérèse de l'Enfant-Jésus et de la Sainte-Face,* texts complied by Sr. Cécile and Sr Geneviève (Paris: Cerf and Desclée de Brouwer, 1979), 70–94.

27   PA 474.

28   See *The Raccolta* # 423 (London: Burns and Oates, 1915), 367–368.

Chapter Five: The Eucharist

1   *Rule* new numbering # 14 (traditional chapter 10).

2   See K. Waaijman, *The Mystical Space of Carmel: A Commentary on the
     Carmelite Rule.* The Fiery Arrow 1 (Leuven: Peeters, 1999), 115–119; C.
     Cicconnetti, *La regola del Carmelo: Origine – natura – significato.* Textus
     et studia historica carmelitana 12 (Rome: Institutum Carmelitanum,
     1973), 399–401.

3   See E. Day, 'Communion, Frequency of' in *New Catholic Encyclopedia*
     (Washington: Catholic University of America, 1967), 4:35–37.

4   *Constitutions,* London 1281, # 20; Bordeaux 1294, # 16.

5   SSoul ch. 5, 104/Ms A 48v, OeuvC 148/CritEd 157.

6   T. Bierle, *Das eucharistische Leben der heiligen Therese von Lisieux*
     (Leutesdorf: Johannes-Verlag, 1982); L. Guillet, 'Thérèse et
     l'Eucharistie,' *Vie thérésienne* 21 (1981), 87–196.

7   SSoul ch. 8, 172/Ms A 79v, OeuvC 204/CritEd 215.

8   Deposition of Mother Agnes at beatification process, PO 152.

9   LastConv from Sr Marie of the Sacred Heart, July/262, OeuvC 1182,
     found also in Sr. Marie's testimony, PO 249.

10   *Sacra tridentina synodus* (20 December 1905); Latin text DS 3375–3383.

11   *Catechism of the Catholic Church,* # 1388.

12   *Code of Canon Law,* can. 917; a clarification the following year restricted
     the reception to twice in the one day, see AAS 76(1984), 746.

13   SSoul ch. 3, 57/Ms A 25v, OeuvC 108/CritEd 114–115.

14   SSoul ch. 4, 74/Ms A 33r, OeuvC 121–122/CritEd 128–129.

15   SSoul ch. 4, 74/Ms A 33r, OeuvC 121–122/CritEd 129.

16   See A. Laforest, *The Way to Love: Thérèse of Lisieux* (Franklin Wis.: 2000),
     19–23.

17   SSoul ch. 4, 77/Ms A 35r, OeuvC 125/CritEd 132. On this text see A.
     Guny, 'Eucharistie et expérience spiritualle chez Sainte Thérèse de
     l'Enfant-Jésus,' *Vie thérésienne* 18 (1978), 254–273 at 256–260; L.
     Guillet, 'Thérèse et l'Eucharistie', ch. 5, 135–146.

18   SSoul ch. 4, 77–78/Ms A 35r-v, OeuvC 125/CritEd 132–133.

19   SSoul ch. 2, 49/Ms A 22r, OeuvC 103/CritEd 109.

20   SSoul ch. 4, 78/Ms A 35v, OeuvC 125–126/CritEd 133.

21   See SSoul ch. 4, 79–80/Ms A 36r-37r, OeuvC 126–128/CritEd
     133–135; see also C. O'Donnell, *Love in the Heart of the Church,* ch. 5,
     esp. 86–98 with studies in nn. 1, 4 and 40.

22   See SSoul ch. 4, 84, 88–89, 93/Ms A 39r, 41v, 44r, OeuvC 132–133,
     136, 140/CritEd 139,143, 147.

23   Her letter in Letters 1:565–566, in part OeuvC 1308.

24   C. De Meester, *The Power of Confidence: Genesis and Structure of the 'Way
     of Spiritual Childhood' of Saint Thérèse* of Lisieux, translated from revised
     edition (New York: Alba House, 1998), 361-365 at 364.

25   See Letters 1:569, n. 4.

26   LT 92/Letters 1:567–568, OeuvC 393, ellipsis points and emphasis of Thérèse.

27   LT 92/Letters 1:568–569, OeuvC 394.

28   SSoul ch. 8, 173/Ms A 80r, OeuvC 205/CritEd 216–217.

29   SSoul ch. 8, 173/Ms A 80r, OeuvC 205/CritEd 216.

30   See SSoul ch. 10, 205–206/Ms C-G, 2v-3r, OeuvC 237–238/CritEd 251–253.

31   SSoul ch. 8, 172/Ms A 79v, OeuvC 204/CritEd 216.

32   SSoul ch. 8, 172–173/Ms A 79v–80r, OeuvC 204–205/CritEd 216.

33   See St John of the Cross, *Ascent of Mount Carmel,* 1:13–15, with 1:15, 3 indicating freedom.

34   LT 165/Letters 2:863, OeuvC 499. See PN 17:1 and 4/89, 90, OeuvC 667–668 for the images of visiting and of the tent at the Transfiguration and comment by C. De Meester, Crit. Ed. 216, n. 315.

35   For example, A. Guéranger, *The Liturgical Year: Lent* (London: Burns, Oates and Washbourne, 1930), 96 (preparation), 98 (thanksgiving).

36   See Geneviève Devergnies, 'A Day in Carmel' in *Saint Thérèse of Lisieux: Her Life, Times and Teaching,* ed. C. De Meester (Washington: ICS, 1997), 131.

37   *The Roman Missal: General Instruction,* # 56 j).

38   'On Developing Eucharistic Devotion' in *Mission and Grace: Essays in Pastoral Theology,* vol. 1 (London: Sheed and Ward, 1963, from German 1959,1961), 276–325 at 285.

39   SSoul ch. 8, 165/Ms A 75v–76r, OeuvC 197/CritEd 208; the scripture quotation is Ps 102:14.

40   SSoul ch. 2, 38/Ms A 15r, OeuvC 92–93/CritEd 98.

41   See LastConv 20,8,10n/157, OeuvC 1099n.

42   LastConv 15.7.1/98, OeuvC 1044–1055.

43   SSoul, ch. 11, 254/Ms C-G 33v-34r, OeuvC 280–281/CritEd 299–300.

44   See SSoul ch. 9, 194/Ms B-M 3v, OeuvC 226/CritEd 331–332

45   C. De Meester, CritEd 300, n. 124 and 329, n. 26. She generally uses the polite *vous* in the *Story of a Soul,* except for the letter to Marie, MS B-M, which is written as an address to Jesus, that her sister is invited to overhear. The intimate *tu-ton-toi* are more common in her poetry.

46   John Paul II, apostolic letter, *Divini amoris scientia* (1997); see C. O'Donnell, 'Thérèse Among Doctors of the Church', Milltown *Studies* 45 (2000) 43-69, esp. 59–60.

47   LT 189/Letters 2:957, OeuvC 538. See also LT 189, 201, 226/Letters 2:956, 1016, 1094, OeuvC 537, 559, 589.

48   SSoul ch. 11, 251/Ms C-G 31v, OeuvC 277/CritEd 296.

49   PN 25:6–8/134–135, OeuvC 702–703.

50   PN, p. 133, n. 1.

51   M. Diego Sánchez, 'La liturgia teresiano-lexoviense: Aproximación desde la liturgia carmelitana' in AA.VV. *Teresa di Lisieux: Novità e grandezza di un dottorato* (Rome: Teresianum, 2000), 345–385 at 356–366.

52   *The Carmelite Missal* (Carmelite Order: private circulation, 1979), 42.

53   Ibid., 141.

54   Diego Sánchez, 'La liturgia', 365.

55   *Carmelite Missal,* 43.

Chapter Six: Mental Prayer and Praying with Scripture

1   *Catechism of the Catholic Church* (Dublin: Veritas, 1994), ## 2705–2708.

2   Ibid., # 2708.

3   Ibid., # 2723.

4   Ibid., # 2709.

5   SSoul, ch. 2, 37/Ms A 14v, OeuvC 91/CritEd 97.

6   Catechism, # 2706.

7   SSoul ch. 4, 74/Ms A 33r, OeuvC 122/CritEd 129.

8   SSoul ch. 4, 91/Ms A 43r, OeuvC 138/CritEd 145.

9   SSoul ch. 7, 158/Ms A 73v-74r, OeuvC 194/CritEd 205.

10   SSoul ch. 5, 102/Ms A 47r, OeuvC 146/CritEd 153; see also ch. 8, 179/Ms A 83v, OeuvC 211/CritEd 224.

11   SSoul ch. 8, 179/Ms A 83r, OeuvC 210/CritEd 224.

12   SSoul ch. 7, 158/Ms A 74r, OeuvC 194/CritEd 205.

13   SSoul ch. 10, 220/Ms C–G 12r, OeuvC 250/CritEd 268. See LT 160 and 193/Letters 2: 848 and 978, OeuvC 491 and 547; PN 54:2 and 7/Poems 215, 216, OeuvC 750, 751.

14   LT 193/Letters 2:978, OeuvC 547.

15   SSoul ch. 8, 179/Ms A 83r–v, OeuvC 210–211/CritEd 224–225.

16   SSoul ch. 5, 102/Ms A 47r, OeuvC 146/CritEd 153.

17   See *Spiritual Exercises,* 'Rules for the Discernment of Spirits', ## 329–336.

18   See *La Bible avec Thérèse de Lisieux: Textes de sainte Thérèse de l'Enfant-Jésus et de la Sainte-Face.* Complied by Sr Cécile and Sr Geneviève (Paris: Cerf and Desclée de Brouwer, 1979) with important introduction by Mgr G. Gaucher 9–41; see also art. 'Sacrada escritura' in P. Teixeira Cavalcante, *Dicionário de santa Teresinha: Pequena enciclopédia sobre santa Teresinha* (São Paulo: Paulus, 1997), 477–480; R. Llamas, 'La biblia fuente espiritual en la vida y el mensaje de s. Teresa de Lisieux', *Ephemerides carmeliticae* 32 (1981), 125–153; Fr Marie-Philippe, 'Thérèse et la Parole de Dieu', *Vives flammes* 222 (1996), 16–31; M. Veys, 'Thérèse et la bible', Carmel (Venasque) 19 (1980), 129–138;

19 Apostolic letter, *Divini amoris scientia,* # 9 in *L'Osservatore Romano* (English edition), 29 October 1997.

20 O'Mahony, 122–123/PO 275. See also CS ch. 3, 72–73/ch. 4 107–108 and LastConv 4,8,5/132, OeuvC 1076.

21 See all texts in previous note.

22 SSoul ch. 10, 208/Ms C–G 3r, OeuvC 237–238/CritEd 252.

23 '. . . ces quelques pages lui furent un aliment délicieux pour ses oraisons' in CS ch. 3, 72/Ch. 4, 107.

24 See CS 72, n. 2/108, n. 8.

25 PO 411/O'Mahony 204; see also PA 349–350.

26 Marie de la Trinité et de la Sainte-Face in PO 462.

27 CS ch. 3, 71–72/4, 107. See also testimony of her sister Léonie PO 352.

28 'Mais surtout ce qui l'occupait, pendent les oraisons, c'était la méditation du Saint Évangile.' PO 275; see O'Mahony 122.

29 '[Elle] faisait ses délices de la sainte Écriture; elle n'était jamais embarrassée dans la choix des passages qui convenaient le mieux aux âmes; on voyait qu'elle en faisait chaque jour l'aliment de sa vie intérieure.' PA 330.

30 *Rule* new numbering # 10 (traditional ch. 7).

31 SSoul ch. 10, 209/Ms C–G 4r, OeuvC 239/CritEd 254.

32 SSoul ch. 5, 99/Ms A 45v, OeuvC 143/CritEd 150.

33 SSoul ch. 6, 133/Ms A 62v, OeuvC 174/CritEd 183.

34 *Interior Castle* 6:3, 5–7 in *Collected Works of St Teresa of Avila,* trans. K. Kavanaugh and O. Rodriguez (Washington DC: ICS, 1980), 2:372–373.

35 Another example LT 230/Letters 2:1101, OeuvC 592.

36 SSoul ch. 10, 208/Ms C–G 3r, OeuvC 237–238/CritEd 252.

37 SSoul ch. 9, 193–194/Ms B–M 3r–v, OeuvC 225–226/CritEd 330–331

38 LT 143/Letters 2:800, OeuvC 466.

39 LT 143/Letters 2:801, OeuvC 466–467.

40 SSoul ch. 113/Ms A 2r, OeuvC 71/CritEd 75–76.

41 SSoul ch. 4, 79/Ms A 36r, OeuvC 126-127/CritEd 134.

42 SSoul ch. 4, 79/Ms A 36v, OeuvC 127/CritEd 134.

43 SSoul ch. 11, 254–259 at 254/Ms C–G 33v–37r, OeuvC 281–285 at 281/CritEd 300–305 at 300.

44 SSoul ch. 10, 219/Ms C–G 11v, OeuvC 249/CritEd 267.

45. SSoul ch. 10, 220–229/Ms C–G 12r–18v, OeuvC 249–259/CritEd 267–277.

46 SSoul ch. 10, 228/Ms C–G 17v, OeuvC 258/CritEd 276.

47 LT 165/Letters 2:861, OeuvC 498.

48 *La Bible avec Ste Thérèse,* 34.

Chapter Seven: Prayers of Thérèse

1   S. Payne, 'Editor's Preface' to *The Prayers of Saint Thérèse of Lisieux*, trans.
     A. Kane (Washington DC: ICS, 1997), 7.

2   SSoul ch. 11, 242–243/Ms C–G 25r–25v, OeuvC 268–269/CritEd
     287–288.

3   See SSoul ch. 5, 99–101/Ms A 45v–46v, OeuvC 143–144/CritEd
     151–152.

4   CritEd 287, n. 101; see *Living Flame* 2:31.

5   LT 171/Letters 2:888, OeuvC 509–510.

6   LT 131/Letters 2:739, OeuvC 442.

7   See LT 131, 150, 152, 178, 255 etc. See Letters 2:911, n. 10.

8   PN 38/167–168, OeuvC 722–723.

9   PO 519.

10   SSoul ch. 11, 242/Ms C–G 25r, OeuvC 268/CritEd 287.

11   *Life* 8:5 in *Collected Works*, trans. K. Kavanaugh and O. Rodriguez, 3
     Vols. (Washington: ICS, 1976–1985) 1:67.

12   SSoul ch. 11, 242/Ms C–G 25r–v, OeuvC 268/CritEd 287.

13   See Interior Castle, 'Fourth Mansions', chapter one.

14   Ibid. 4:1, 5.

15   SSoul ch. 5, 115; ch. 6, 123; ch. 8, 170; ch. 8, 173/ Ms A 54r; 57r; 78v;
     80r, OeuvC 159, 165, 202, 205/CritEd 168, 174, 213–214, 217.

16   Apostolic exhortation, *Marialis cultus* ('To Honour Mary') # 55.

17   See C. O'Donnell, 'Living by Faith', *Love in the Heart of the Church: The
     Mission of St Thérèse of Lisieux* (Dublin: Veritas, 1997), 166–185 with
     notes 244–248.

18   PO 151–152. See also RP 7:1v, OeuvC 916; SSoul ch. 8, 165,179/Ms A
     75v–76r, 83r, OeuvC 197–198, 210/CritEd 208, 224.

19   PO 272.

20   See J. de Guibert, *The Theology of the Spiritual Life* (London: Sheed and
     Ward, 1954, from Latin text posthumously published in 1946),
     220–222; A. Tanquerey, *The Spiritual Life: A Treatise on Ascetical and
     Mystical Theology* (Tournai: Desclée, 2nd ed. 1930), 925–929.

21   SSoul ch. 11, 243/Ms C-G 25v, OeuvC 269/CritEd 288.

22   *Way of Perfection* 21:8 in *Collected Works* 2:120; see also 21:3, p. 118.

23   Ibid., chs. 27–42.

24   Ibid., 25:3, p. 132.

25   SSoul ch. 8, 165/Ms A 76r, OeuvC 197–198/CritEd 208.

26   LT 82, 83, 85–87, 89.

27   LT 94/Letters 1:577, OeuvC 396.

28   Interior Castle 2:1, 8 in *Collected Works* 2:301.

29   LT 36/Letters 1:353, OeuvC 329.

30   SSoul ch. 6, 136/Ms A 64r–v, OeuvC 177–178/CritEd 186–187.

31 Pri 1, 37, OeuvC 957.

32 See SSoul ch. 3, 65–67 and ch. 6, 123/Ms A 30r–31r, 56v, OeuvC 116–118, 164/CritEd 122–125, 174.

33 Pri 21, 119 with facsimile 36, OeuvC 976.

34 Ibid., 119–120.

35 'General Introduction,' Pri 16-22.

36 Pri 10, 86, OeuvC 968.

37 Pri 2, 38, OeuvC 957-958.

38 See Pri 53–74 and authors cited there; C. De Meester, *I Offer Myself to Your Love: Commentary on Thérèse of Lisieux's Offering to Merciful Love* (Strasbourg: Éditons du Signe, 1999); C. De Meester, 'The Offering to Merciful Love' in *St Thérèse of Lisieux: Her Life, Times and Teaching,* ed. C. De Meester (Washington: ICS, 1997), 155-162; G. Emonnet, *L'offrande thérésienne aujourd'hui* (Paris: Apostolat des Editions, 1976); A. Bandera, 'La ofrenda de Santa Teresa del Niño Jesús al Amor Misericordiosa,' *La vida sobonatural* 64 (1984), 5–14; more briefly O'Donnell, *Love in the Heart of the Church* 37–43.

39 Pri 12, 91, OeuvC 969; the quotation is St John of the Cross, *Spiritual Canticle* 29:2.

40 SSoul ch. 7, 152/Ms A 71r, OeuvC 189/CritEd 200.

41 SSoul ch. 11, 251–254/Ms C–G 31v-33v, OeuvC 277–281/CritEd 295–299.

42 Rule new numbering ##18–19 (traditional ch. 14).

43 Pri 8, 78–79, OeuvC 966–967.

Chapter Eight: Thérèse Still Guides US

1 SSoul ch. 11, 258/Ms C–G 35r–36v, OeuvC 284/CritEd 304 (translation slightly modified in final lines).

2 M. Frohlich, 'Desolation and Doctrine in Thérèse of Lisieux', Theological Studies 61(2000) 261–279.

3 LastConv 13,7,17/ 94–95, OeuvC 1042.

4 SSoul ch. 9, 197/Ms B–M 4v, OeuvC 229/CritEd 336.

5 SSoul ch. 9, 198–200/Ms B–M 4v–5v, OeuvC 229–232/CritEd 336–341 with important nn. 53, 63, 64, 66.

6 SSoul ch. 9, 198/Ms B–M 5r, OeuvC 229/CritEd 336.

7 SSoul ch. 9, 200/Ms B–M 5v, OeuvC 231/CritEd 340.

8 CS ch. 2,56-57/42–43.

9 SSoul ch. 8, 179/Ms A 83v, OeuvC 211/CritEd 224.

10 SSoul ch. 7, 151/Ms A 71r, OeuvC 189/CritEd 199; see also ch. 7, 158; ch. 8, 173/Ms A 74r; 80v, OeuvC 195, 205/CritEd 205–206, 217.

11 LT 142/Letters 2:796, OeuvC 464–465.

12   Apostolic letter, *Divini amoris scientia* (19 October 1997) # 7.
13   See Vatican II on charism, especially Constitution on the Church, LG 12.
14   Vatican II, *Constitution on the Church,* LG 9.
15   SSoul ch. 6, 142–143/Ms A 68r, OeuvC 184/CritEd 193.
16   See C. O'Donnell, *Love in the Heart of the Church: The Mission of Thérèse of Lisieux* (Dublin: Veritas, 1997) 137–153 with works cited 238–241 and add P. Ahern, *Maurice and Thérèse: The Story of a Love* (New York: Doubleday, 1998; London: Darton, Longman and Todd, 1999).
17   Pri 91–98 at 93–94.
18   Pri 53–74.
19   SSoul ch. 8, 180/MS A 83v–84r, OeuvC 211–212/CritEd 225–228.
20   For text see SSoul 276–277, OeuvC 962–964/Pri 6, 53–55.
21   See *Letters* 2:1000, n. 6.
22   Pri 63–64.
23   7,7,2; 29,7,9; 8,8,2/77, 117,141, OeuvC, 1026-1027, 1064, 1085.
24   SSoul ch. 9, 200/Ms B–M 5v, OeuvC 232/CritEd 241.
25   CritEd 341, n. 70.
26   SSoul ch. 9, 192/Ms B–M 3r, OeuvC 224/CritEd 329.
27   Text in B. Edwards, trans. and ed., *The Institutes of the First Monks* (privately published by Carmelite Friars, Boars Hill, Oxford, 1969) 1:2, pp. 3–4.
28   See *Ascent of Mount Carmel,* Prologue, especially nn. 4–6.
29   See Life 17:5 in *Collected Works,* translated by K. Kavanaugh and O. Rodriguez (Washington: ICS, 1976-1985) 1:103.
30   'The Spirituality of the Church of the Future' in *Theological Investigations.* Vol. 20 (London: Darton, Longman and Todd, 1981) 143–153 at 149; also vol. 7, p. 15; on mysticism see also the collected essays in *The Practice of Faith: A Handbook of Contemporary Spirituality* (New York: Crossroad, 1983) 69–84.
31   SSoul ch. 5, 113/Ms A 53r, OeuvC 157/CritEd 166.
32   *Interior Castle* 4,1,7 in Collected Works 3:319.
33   Ibid. 4:2,8 in *Collected Works* 3:319.
34   MS B–M, usually chapter nine of SSoul.
35   LT 197/Letters 2:1000, OeuvC 553.
36   SSoul ch. 9, 194/MS B–M, 3v, OeuvC 226/CritEd 332.
37   SSoul ch. 11, 242/MS C–G, 25r–v, OeuvC 268/CritEd 287.